SECOND EDITION

TOP NOTCH
2

D0521140

1503-02

Workbook

Joan Saslow • Allen Ascher

With Terra Brockman and Julie C. Rouse

PEARSON
Longman

1503-09

Top Notch: English for Today's World 2, Second Edition
Workbook

Copyright © 2011 by Pearson Education, Inc.
All rights reserved.

No part of this publication may be reproduced,
stored in a retrieval system, or transmitted
in any form or by any means, electronic, mechanical,
photocopying, recording, or otherwise,
without the prior permission of the publisher.

Pearson Education, 10 Bank Street, White Plains, NY 10606

Staff credits: The people who made up the *Top Notch 2 Workbook* team, representing editorial, design, production, and manufacturing, are Rhea Banker, Peter Benson, Elizabeth Carlson, Diane Cipollone, Aerin Csigay, Dave Dickey, Aliza Greenblatt, Ray Keating, Mike Kemper, and Barbara Sabella.

Cover design: Rhea Banker
Cover photo: Sprint / Corbis
Text design: Wendy Wolf
Text composition: Quarasan!
Text font: ITC Stone Sans

Photo credits: All original photography by David Mager. Page 1 (top left) Will & Deni McIntyre/ Getty Images, (top middle left) Michael Goldman/Masterfile, (top middle right) P. Sheandell/age fotostock, (top right) Jeff Greenberg/PhotoEdit Inc.; p. 4 Angelo Cavalli/Index Stock Imagery; p. 7 Shutterstock.com; p. 14 Shutterstock.com; p. 18 Shutterstock.com; p. 22 Shutterstock.com; p. 24 Fredde Lieberman; p. 32 Shutterstock.com; p. 39 Shutterstock.com; p. 45 Shutterstock.com; p. 49 Shutterstock.com; p. 50 Getty Images; p. 51 Shutterstock.com; p. 66 Index Stock Imagery; p. 67 (sombrero) Shutterstock.com, (bag) David Young-Wolff/PhotoEdit, (elephant figure) Shutterstock. com, (rocking chair) Shutterstock.com, (balalaika) Shutterstock.com, (vase) The Art Archive/Dagli Orti; p. 68 Shutterstock.com; p. 69 (Picasso) Bettmann/Corbis, (Pollock) Rudolph Burckhardt/Sygma/ Corbis, (Matisse) Bettmann/Corbis; p. 70 The Gallery Collection/Corbis; p. 74 Shutterstock.com; p. 77 Shutterstock.com; p. 79 Shutterstock.com; p. 89 AP Images/Stephen J. Carrera.

Illustration credits: Steve Attoe: pages 5 (top), 24, 46, 87 (top); Mark Collins: page 17; Leeanne Franson: pages 3, 5 (bottom), 29, 87 (bottom 4); Brian Hughes: pages 30, 37; Stephen Hutchings: page 20; Suzanne Mogensen: pages 18, 19, 48; Andy Myer: page 10; Dusan Petriçic: pages 25, 33, 86; Neil Stewart: page 42; Anne Veltfort: page 38.

ISBN 13: 978-0-13-247052-0
ISBN 10: 0-13-247052-7

Printed in the United States of America
1 2 3 4 5 6 7 8 9 10 –V042—15 14 13 12 11 10

PEARSON LONGMAN ON THE WEB

Pearsonlongman.com offers online resources for teachers and students. Access our Companion Websites, our online catalog, and our local offices around the world.

Visit us at **www.pearsonlongman.com**.

CONTENTS

Photocopy
workbook.
for homework.

Greetings and Small Talk

1 Look at the pictures. Write the correct greeting under each picture. Use words from the box.

| bow | hug | kiss | shake hands |

1. _____

2. _____

3. _____

4. _____

2 Complete the conversation. Write the letter on the line.

A: You look familiar. Haven't we met before?

B: _____
1.

A: Aren't you from Canada?

B: _____
2.

A: I know! I think we met at Joan's house last month.

B: _____
3.

A: Yes, that's right. What have you been up to?

B: _____
4.

A: Well, it was nice to see you again.

B: _____
5.

A: That would be great. Here's my card.

a. Of course! You work with Joan.

b. You, too. We should keep in touch.

c. Not much. Actually, I'm on my way to a class.

d. I don't think so. I'm not from around here.

e. Yes, I am. I'm from Vancouver.

3 Read the conversation in Exercise 2 again. Circle the subjects the people talk about.

family   religion   job   age   weather   nationality

4 When you meet someone new, what subjects do you talk about? Write a ✔ next to the topics you usually talk about. Write an ✗ next to the topics you don't like to talk about.

_____ 1. my family

_____ 2. my religion

_____ 3. the weather

_____ 4. my age

_____ 5. my hometown or country

_____ 6. sports

_____ 7. politics

_____ 8. my job

_____ 9. other: _____

1

5 Complete each sentence with the present perfect. Use contractions when possible.

1. A: _____ any coffee today?
   <u>you / have</u>
   B: Yes, _____ two cups.
   <u>I / have</u>

2. A: _____ to Europe?
   <u>you / be</u>
   B: Yes, _____ to Spain.
   <u>we / be</u>

3. A: _____ this week?
   <u>you / exercise</u>
   B: Yes, _____ to the gym twice.
   <u>I / go</u>

4. A: _____ any books lately?
   <u>you / read</u>
   B: No, _____ too busy.
   <u>I / be</u>

6 Complete the questions with the correct form of the verbs from the box.
Use each verb only once. Then write your own responses. When you answer <u>yes</u>,
add specific information, using the simple past tense.

| be | check | eat | meet | ~~see~~ |

1. "Have you _seen_ any good movies lately?"
   YOU _Yes, I have. I saw Toy Story 3 last week._

2. "Have you _____ any famous people?"
   YOU _____

3. "Have you _____ to Europe?"
   YOU _____

4. "Have you _____ lunch today?"
   YOU _____

5. "Have you _____ your e-mail today?"
   YOU _____

7 Complete the conversation with the present perfect or the simple past tense.
Use contractions when possible.

Joe: _____ this tour before? I hear it's great.
     <u>1. you / take</u>

Trish: Yes, I have. I _____ to Russia with this group two years ago.
       <u>2. come</u>

     It _____ a wonderful trip. _____ here before?
        <u>3. be</u>   <u>4. you / be</u>

Joe: Yes, I _____ Moscow in 2005, but I _____ much of the city.
            <u>5. visit</u>   <u>6. not / see</u>

     It _____ a business trip. I'm really excited about *this* trip!
        <u>7. be</u>

Trish: Me too. I _____ the brochures several times last night. I can't wait to see all
                <u>8. read</u>

     these places again. By the way, _____ Peter, our tour guide?
                                      <u>9. you / meet</u>

Joe: No, but I'd like to.

Trish: Come. I'll introduce you.

8 **Complete the sentences. Circle the correct words.**

1. Have you visited the Louvre (yet / ever)?

2. I haven't been to the opera (already / yet).

3. Who is she? I haven't (ever / before) seen her.

4. Has Evan (yet / ever) tried ceviche (already / before)?

5. We've only been here one day, but we've (already / yet) taken a lot of pictures.

6. My parents have been to Italy (ever / before).

7. Has she (yet / ever) gone sightseeing in New York?

8. Have they (already / before) seen the new Brad Pitt movie?

9 **Complete the conversations. Write questions or answers in the present perfect. Use <u>already</u>, <u>yet</u>, <u>ever</u>, or <u>before</u>.**

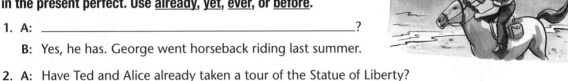

1. **A:** _____?
   B: Yes, he has. George went horseback riding last summer.

2. **A:** Have Ted and Alice already taken a tour of the Statue of Liberty?
   B: No. They _____.

3. **A:** _____?
   B: Yes. I've been to London several times.

4. **A:** _____?
   B: No, but they plan to go to the top of the Sears Tower tomorrow.

5. **A:** Has Lisa ever tried Turkish coffee?
   B: Yes. She _____.

10 **Look at Anne Marie and Gilbert's to-do list for their vacation in Toronto. Anne Marie has checked what they have already done.**

> ✓ – take a tour of the university
> ✓ – meet Michel for dinner on Spadina Avenue
>   – visit the Bata Shoe Museum
> ✓ – see a musical downtown
>   – take a boat trip around Toronto Harbor
> ✓ – go shopping at the Eaton Centre

Now finish Anne Marie's postcard to her friend. Write what she and Gilbert have already done and what they haven't done yet. Use the present perfect.

Dear Agnes,   Sunday, August 6

Gilbert and I are having a wonderful time in Toronto.
We've done so many things! _____
_____
_____
_____
_____
_____
_____

See you when we get back.

Love,
Anne Marie

LESSON 3

11

Extra reading comprehension

Read the article on page 8 in the Student's Book again. Answer the questions.

1. What is "body talk"? _____

2. How should you greet someone in France? _____

3. Where is hugging common during introductions? _____

4. What does the "OK" sign mean in Japan? _____

5. What advice does the article give? _____

12 **Read the information about greetings in Asia. Then read the statements and check true, false, or no information.**

> ## GETTING GREETINGS RIGHT
>
> The traditional greeting in Asia is a bow. In fact, there are different types of bows used in greetings throughout Asia. For example, in Japan, China, and Korea, people bow, but in Japan the bow is usually lower. In India and nearby countries in South Asia, most people put their hands together and bow just a little.
>
> While each Asian culture has its own traditional special greeting, these days, don't be surprised if people in Asia just shake your hand.

	true	false	no information
1. People in China, Japan, and Korea bow when they greet someone.	☐	☐	☐
2. In Korea, people usually bow lower than in Japan.	☐	☐	☐
3. In India, you shouldn't touch the person you are greeting.	☐	☐	☐
4. People in many places in South Asia use a similar greeting.	☐	☐	☐

13 **Complete the sentences about yourself.**

1. In this country, the most common greeting is _____.

2. When I greet someone for the first time, I usually _____.

3. When I greet a family member or close friend, I usually _____.

FACTOID

History of the Handshake
Shaking hands was a way of making sure that people were not carrying a weapon such as a knife or sword. When you shook hands, you were saying, "Look, I don't have a weapon. I trust you. Let's be friends."

LESSON 4

14 **Complete the chart. Write things you've done and things you haven't done but would like to do.**

KILIMANJARO →

	Things I've done	Things I'd like to do
climb	climb Mt. Kilimanjaro	climb Mt. Everest

	Things I've done	Things I'd like to do
climb		
visit		
go sightseeing in		
learn		
go to the top of		
see		
try		
meet		
take a tour of		

15 CHALLENGE. Look at your experiences in Exercise 14. Write about three things you've done using **already** or **before**. Describe each experience with a participial adjective.

I've already climbed Mt. Kilimanjaro in Tanzania. It was thrilling!

1. _____
2. _____
3. _____

Now write about three things you haven't done but would like to do. Use **yet**, **have never**, or **haven't ever**.

1. _____
2. _____
3. _____

GRAMMAR BOOSTER

A Look at the answers. Write information questions, using the question words in parentheses.

1. **A:** (Where) _____?
   B: He's lived in Santiago, Budapest, and Kyoto.

2. **A:** (How) _____?
   B: It's been great—sunny and warm every day!

3. **A:** (What) _____?
   B: Sophie has studied English, Spanish, and Japanese.

4. **A:** (Which) _____?
   B: They've gone to the Metropolitan Museum of Art and the Museum of Modern Art.

5. **A:** (How many) _____?
   B: She's been to Paris three times.

6. **A:** (Who) _____?
   B: I've met Mr. Russ, Mr. Sherman, and Ms. Savidge.

B Rewrite each sentence, changing the placement of **yet** or **already**.

1. We've taken that tour already. _____
2. They haven't yet climbed Mt. McKinley. _____
3. Has he eaten dinner already? _____
4. I've already gone sightseeing in Prague. _____
5. She hasn't tried Vietnamese food yet. _____

C Complete the sentences. Circle the correct words.

City of Arts and Sciences—Valencia, Spain

1. Have you (yet / already) taken pictures of the City of Arts and Sciences building?
2. Josefina hasn't had her lunch (yet / already).
3. Ryan has finished college (yet / already).
4. Has Michelle (ever / before) been to Greece?
5. My parents have (ever / never) gone on a cruise.
6. I haven't (ever / never) studied Italian.
7. Ruth has (ever / never) tried duck before.
8. Simone is from Paris, but she's never (ever / before) gone to the top of the Eiffel Tower!

D Think of a frightening, a thrilling, a fascinating, and a disgusting experience. Write questions with <u>ever</u>.

> 1. frightening: *Have you ever jumped out of an airplane?*

1. frightening: _____
2. thrilling: _____
3. fascinating: _____
4. disgusting: _____

Now write short answers to your questions.

1. _____   3. _____
2. _____   4. _____

E CHALLENGE. What are four things that you've never done? Write sentences using the words in parentheses.

1. (never) _____
2. (not ever) _____
3. (never, before) _____
4. (never, ever) _____

A Read the run-on sentences. Write each sentence correctly. Separate the independent clauses with a period or combine them with a coordinating conjunction, such as <u>and</u> or <u>but</u>.

1. My parents went on a cruise to the Bahamas they haven't been to Bermuda yet.

   _____

   _____

2. I've been to the top of the CN Tower, the view is amazing.

   _____

   _____

3. They went skiing in the Himalayas, the trip was thrilling.

   _____

   _____

4. I've tried snails before they were disgusting.

   _____

   _____

5. Devin has never traveled to continental Europe he has visited Ireland before.

   _____

   _____

6. We have met before we were on the same sightseeing tour yesterday.

   _____

   _____

7. He's from Russia, he has studied English, he would like to learn Mandarin.

   _____

   _____

B Look at Exercise C on page 11 in the Student's Book. On a separate sheet of paper, write your partner's experience. Describe what happened, where your partner was, who your partner was with, and how he or she felt.

C After you write about your partner's experience in Exercise B, check to see if you have written any run-on sentences. Be sure to use a period to separate the independent clauses or use connecting words to combine them.

Movies and Entertainment

1 Complete the sentences with words or expressions from the box.

a bunch of	Frankly	I can't stand	It's my treat	I've heard

1. There are _____ good new comedies on Netclips. I can't decide which one to watch.

2. _____ the new Leonardo DiCaprio movie is fantastic. Have you seen it yet?

3. I have two tickets for the 10:00 show. Would you like to go? _____.

4. *Titanic?* _____, I'm too tired for a three-hour romantic epic!

5. _____ horror movies. I watch movies to relax—not to be frightened.

2 Answer the questions about your own movie preferences.

1. What actor or actress are you a big fan of? _____

2. What movie genres are you usually in the mood for? _____

3. What was the last movie you saw in a theater? _____

4. What was the last movie you watched at home? _____

LESSON 1

3 Complete the posting from an online movie message board. Use <u>since</u> or <u>for</u>.

➡ Movie Reviews

Back   Forward   Reload   Stop   Home   Search

ONLINE MOVIE REVIEWS

Actors
Links
Schedule
Discussion Board

Name: Veeck

Date: 7/10 8:12 A.M.

Post # 5

Comments: I've been an action film fan _____ 20 years,
1.
_____ I was 10 years old. I haven't seen a good one
2.
_____ a very long time. Last night I saw the movie *Robin
3.
Hood* and it was terrible. I watched it for about an hour but
then I had to turn it off. I kept falling asleep!! It was the worst
action film I've seen _____ 1991, when I saw *Rambo*.
4.
In my opinion, there still haven't been any good action films
_____ *Avatar* in 2009. What a disappointment!
5.

4 Look at the pictures. Then complete the conversation.

Patty: Hi, Rosemary. Sorry I'm late. Have you been here long?

Rosemary: For about twenty minutes. What happened?

Patty: First _____. I ran to catch it, but it pulled away. And
1.
_____, because it was raining. So, I went back home to get my car.
2.
Then _____. Finally I got here, but _____.
3.   4.
It took me about ten minutes before I found one!

Rosemary: Well, you're here now. Let's go see the movie!

LESSON 2

5 Match each movie genre with the correct description. Write the letter on the line.

1. _____ feature fast-paced, exciting, and dangerous situations   **a.** dramas

2. _____ are drawn by hand or created on a computer   **b.** documentaries

3. _____ tell a story with singing and dancing   **c.** science-fiction films

4. _____ give us information about real people and things   **d.** action films

5. _____ usually take place in the future   **e.** animated films

6. _____ make us smile and laugh   **f.** musicals

7. _____ focus on characters' problems and emotions   **g.** comedies

6 Read the newspaper movie listings. Write the genre that best describes each movie.

ESSEX TIMES

Friday, May 22	ENTERTAINMENT	page 39

The Fearless Fighter 🎥
You'll be on the edge of your seat. Don't miss this exciting adventure! But don't bring the kids—a little too violent.
Edgewood Theater: 6:00, 8:15, 10:30

Myra's Day 🎥
Spend the day with Myra. You'll laugh so hard you might fall out of your seat!
Plaza Cinemas: 4:00, 6:00, 8:00

Goodnight, Mariana 🎥
Mariana tries to find her long lost mother. Her search takes her all over the country. Very sad and touching. Based on a true story.
Castle Theater: 4:00, 6:15, 8:30

Genre: _____   Genre: _____   Genre: _____

7 CHALLENGE. **Which of the movies from the listing in Exercise 6 would you rather see? Explain your answer.**

8 Look at Tom's favorite things and <u>least</u> favorite things. Then read each statement and check <u>true</u> or <u>false</u>, based on Tom's lists.

Tom's Favorite Things

1. comedies
2. a trip to the beach
3. pop music
4. going to the gym
5. rice

Tom's <u>Least</u> Favorite Things

1. documentaries
2. a trip to the mountains
3. classical music
4. going shopping
5. pasta

	true	false
1. Tom would rather see a comedy than a documentary.	☐	☐
2. He'd rather take a trip to the mountains than to the beach.	☐	☐
3. He'd rather listen to classical music than pop music.	☐	☐
4. He'd rather go to the gym than go shopping.	☐	☐
5. Tom would rather eat rice than pasta.	☐	☐

9 Look at the statements in Exercise 8. Write five true statements about your own preferences. Use <u>would rather</u>.

10 Read the online movie reviews. Then complete the chart. Write the genre and choose two adjectives from the box to describe each movie. Circle "thumbs up" if the reviewer recommends the movie or "thumbs down" if he or she doesn't recommend it.

| boring | hilarious | interesting | silly | unforgettable | violent | weird |

Movie title	Genre	Adjectives	Reviewer's opinion
The Alien!			👍 👎
Search for the Lost Kingdom			👍 👎
Dad's Back!			👍 👎
Don't Scream Now			👍 👎

11 Complete the conversation. Write the letter on the line.

A: Hi, Janelle. Seen any good movies recently?

B: _____
1.

A: *Play Time*? What kind of movie is that?

B: _____
2.

A: Well, what is it about?

B: _____
3.

A: That doesn't sound very funny. Was it any good?

B: _____
4.

A: The funniest? Wow! Who was in it?

B: _____
5.

A: So you think I would like it?

B: _____
6.

a. It was terrific. It might be the funniest film I've seen this year.

b. It's a comedy.

c. Definitely. I highly recommend it.

d. Yeah, I just saw *Play Time* at the Art Cinema.

e. It's about some high school kids who don't want to graduate.

f. It stars Wilson Grant—he was really hilarious.

12 CHALLENGE. Write your own review about a movie you've seen. Use the reviews in Exercise 10 for support. In your review, answer the following questions: What kind of movie was it? Who was in it? What was it about? Was it funny? Romantic? Thought-provoking? Would you recommend it?

LESSON 4

13
Extra reading comprehension

Read the article *Can Violent Movies or TV Programs Harm Children?* on page 22 in the Student's Book again. Then read each statement and check <u>true</u> or <u>false</u>, according to the information in the article.

	true	false
1. It's OK for children to watch violence in animated TV shows and movies.	☐	☐
2. Children who watch a lot of fighting and killing on TV are more likely to act violently as adults.	☐	☐
3. Eight is a safe age for children to start watching violent movies and TV shows.	☐	☐
4. Violence is normal, so children should be exposed to it.	☐	☐
5. Children should learn that there are consequences for doing bad things.	☐	☐
6. Parents should watch and discuss violent TV programs with their very young children.	☐	☐

Read the online blog post. Then answer the questions.

○○○

How can I protect my kids from media violence?

08 APR 2011 10:05 PM

POST A COMMENT

James F
view profile

The forecast is for rain all weekend, so I thought I'd get some movies for the kids to watch. When we got to the video store, my nine-year-old son headed straight for the new releases. Every video he picked had a gun or an explosion on the cover. My six-year-old brought me a movie based on one of his favorite toys. He begged me to rent it, "Please, Dad. I have the toys. Why can't I see the movie?" But this movie is not for children. According to the reviews I've read, it's very scary and pretty bloody. We came home with a popular animated film I found in the family section, but even that had fighting in it. And the violent scenes were also silly and funny. Frankly, I think that's sending kids a bad message.

I was so upset that I decided to do some research on children and media violence. Did you know that between the ages of four and eighteen, the average child sees 200,000 acts of violence on TV and other media—including 40,000 murders? Also, 60 to 90% of the most popular video games have violent subject matter. Another study found that 61% of television programs show some violence, and 43% of these violent scenes are used to make people laugh!

Why can't the entertainment industry make kids' movies and TV shows that are actually appropriate for kids? And when will they stop selling toys based on violent movies and video games that young children should not see or play? Maybe next time it rains, I'll take my kids to the library instead!

SOURCE: mediafamily.org

1. What is James F.'s nine-year-old son interested in? _____

2. What does his six-year-old want to see? _____

3. What does James F. rent? _____

4. Why is he upset? _____

5. What does he think the entertainment industry should do? _____

_____

6. Do you agree with James F.? Explain your answer. _____

_____

15 **Complete the statements, according to the blog post in Exercise 14. Circle the letter.**

1. Between the ages of four and eighteen, the average child sees _____ on TV and in other media.
   a. 40,000 television programs   b. 200,000 murders   c. 40,000 murders

2. _____ of all TV shows contain violent scenes.
   a. More than half   b. Half   c. Less than half

3. Violence on TV is often meant to be seen as _____.
   a. unforgettable   b. funny   c. scary

A Read the sentence in column A. Then decide if the sentence in column B is <u>true</u> or <u>false</u>.

A	B	true	false
1. She's been living in Milan for two years.	She still lives in Milan.	☐	☐
2. He's lived in Quito since 2009.	He doesn't live in Quito now.	☐	☐
3. I've climbed Mt. Sorak.	I am climbing Mt. Sorak now.	☐	☐
4. How long have you been reading that book?	You are still reading the book.	☐	☐
5. She's written a review of the new movie.	She's finished writing the review.	☐	☐
6. We've been waiting to see *Avatar*.	We've already seen *Avatar*.	☐	☐

B Think of three activities that you enjoy. When did you start? For each activity, write one present perfect sentence and one present perfect continuous sentence. Use <u>for</u> or <u>since</u>.

I've played the piano for three years. I've been playing the piano for three years.

C Complete each statement with the present perfect continuous.

1. I _____ really good things about the new Keira Knightley movie.
   hear
2. Jimmy _____ me DVDs to watch on the weekends.
   give
3. *Ski Trip* _____ terrible reviews.
   get
4. *Planet X* _____ a lot of money since it came out last week.
   make
5. Audrey's grandparents _____ for her acting classes.
   pay
6. Joe and Clem _____ around Europe and Asia for nine months.
   travel
7. We _____ for a movie for a half hour. Just choose something!
   look

D Complete the sentences. Circle the correct words.

1. I (prefer / would rather) see a silly movie than a violent movie.
2. Annabelle (likes / would rather) classic films.
3. We (prefer / would rather) to order tickets online.
4. She would (like / rather) to watch a romantic comedy.
5. Would you (prefer / rather) sit in the middle or on the aisle?
6. No soda for me. I (prefer / would rather) water.
7. Oscar (prefers / would rather) not go to the movies tonight.

E Look at the answers. Write questions with <u>like</u>, <u>prefer</u>, or <u>would rather</u>. There is more than one correct answer.

1. **A:** _____?

   B: A drama. I'm not that big on musicals.

2. **A:** _____?

   B: Popcorn, please. I don't eat candy.

3. **A:** _____?

   B: Definitely a movie. Plays are fine, but I really love movies.

4. **A:** _____?

   B: Saturday works for me. I'm busy on Sunday.

5. **A:** _____?

   B: I'm not in the mood for Chinese food. What about Mexican?

6. **A:** _____?

   B: It doesn't matter to me. You choose.

WRITING BOOSTER

A Write a topic sentence for the following paragraph.

> **Topic sentence:** _____
>
> People don't imitate the behavior they see in movies. Would you try jumping from the roof of one tall building to another because you saw it in an action film? We live in a violent world. Just open any newspaper—or history book. What happens in real life is more violent than what happens in movies, and violence is not new. Violent entertainment has been around for a long time. Think about the gladiators in ancient Rome.

B Why do some people think violence in movies is harmful? Why do others think it isn't? Complete the chart with people's opinions. Look at Exercise A above and the article on page 22 of the Student's Book for ideas.

Violence in movies	
Harmful	**Not harmful**
Can make children more aggressive	

C On a separate sheet of paper, write two paragraphs of three to five sentences each with details about the following topics. Then write and add a topic sentence for each paragraph.

Paragraph 1

The best movie you ever saw and why you liked it.

Paragraph 2

The worst movie you ever saw and why you couldn't stand it.

Staying in Hotels

1 **Look at the hotel bill. Then answer the questions.**

				ROOM	1631
Mr. Philip Paul				ARRIVAL	09/14
11 Rue Ravignan				DEPARTURE	09/16
Place Emil Goudeau				TIME	15:52
75018 Paris, France					

NOVA HOTEL

CLUB ONE MEMBER # PP2139

DATE	REFERENCE	DESCRIPTION	AMOUNT
9/14	13:13	Local Call	Free (Club One member)
9/14	08:32	Overseas Call	40.34
9/14	3036	Internet access	Free (Club One member)
9/14	2765	Laundry	36.00
9/14		Room 1631	179.00
9/14	3036	Internet access	Free (Club One member)
9/14	2762	Room Service	18.92
9/15	2762	Room Service	26.45
9/15	09:52	Local Call	Free (Club One member)
9/15	428	Photocopies	Free (Club One member)
9/15	3036	Internet access	Free (Club One member)
9/15	758	Local Fax	Free (Club One member)
9/15		Room 1631	179.00
9/15	09562	Airport Shuttle	30.00
		BALANCE	509.71
		VAT 7.00%	35.68
		TOTAL INCLUDING VAT	545.39

1. What date did Mr. Paul check in? _____

2. How much did he pay for phone calls, faxes, and Internet service? _____

3. How many nights did Mr. Paul stay at the hotel? _____

4. What is the total amount of the hotel bill? _____

2 **Check the hotel services that Mr. Paul used at the Nova Hotel, according to the hotel bill.**

☐ ☐ ☐ ☐ ☐

☐ ☐ ☐ ☐ ☐

3 Which services are important to these hotel guests? Read what each person says and write the hotel service on the line.

I like to have breakfast in my room before I get dressed for the day.

1. _____

I need child care so that my wife and I can go out at night.

2. _____

I have a very important meeting in the morning. I can't oversleep!

3. _____

I check e-mail and work on my laptop in the evening.

4. _____

I would rather swim for exercise than lift weights.

5. _____

I want someone to make restaurant and sightseeing reservations for me.

6. _____

LESSON 1

4 Look at the pictures and complete the sentences with **'d better** or **'d better not**.

1. "Hey, look at that sign. We _____
   _____."

2. "Blackbird is a very popular restaurant.
   You _____."

18   UNIT 3

3. "It's after midnight. We _____

_____

_____."

4. "The movie starts in three minutes.

You _____

_____."

5 Complete the conversations. Write responses with <u>had better</u>.

1. **A:** It's 10:45. Check out is at 11:00.

   B: _____

2. **A:** The items in the minibar are really expensive.

   B: _____

3. **A:** Oh, no! I left my purse at the restaurant.

   B: _____

4. **A:** It's a popular movie. Tickets might sell out.

   B: _____

5. **A:** This is a double room. We're a family of five!

   B: _____

6. **A:** The hotel offers a free breakfast, but it's only until 9:00.

   B: _____

7. **A:** The sauna is for adults only.

   B: _____

LESSON 2

6 Put the conversation in order. Write the number on the line.

_1_ Can I speak with Kevin Mercer, please? He's staying in room 376.

____ That's right.

____ Yes. Could you tell him Barbara called? Please ask him to call me back at 555–3156.

____ One moment, please . . . I'm sorry. There's no answer. Can I take a message?

____ Barbara at 555–3156?

____ Is that all?

_7_ Yes, that's it. Thank you very much.

7 The fortune-teller is predicting the future. Read her predictions. Then rewrite the sentences using <u>will</u>.

3. When you are in Barcelona, you meet an old friend.

2. Then, you're taking a trip to Barcelona.

4. Your friend is going to offer you an exciting job in Spain.

1. Next week, you are going to win a prize.

5. Next month, you are moving to Spain.

1. _____

2. _____

3. _____

4. _____

5. _____

8 Rewrite the following future statements and questions using <u>will</u>.

1. I'm going to call her later today. _____

2. She's going to stop at the front desk first. _____

3. My uncle is meeting my father at the airport. _____

4. What time does the tour group get back? _____

5. When are they going to make a reservation? _____

6. Where is your grandmother staying in Madrid? _____

9 Read the phone conversation. Then complete the message sheet.

A: Hello. I'd like to speak with Ms. Marina Santiago, please.

B: One moment, please. I'll ring Ms. Santiago's room . . . I'm sorry, but there's no answer. Would you like to call back later?

A: No, I'd like to leave a message. Please tell her that Anna Streed called. I'll be at 555–8723 until 5:00 today.

B: OK, Ms. Anna Street . . .

A: No, it's Streed, S-T-R-E-E-D—that's "D" as in "door."

B: OK, Ms. Streed. I'll make sure she gets the message.

To <u>Marina Santiago</u>
Date ___<u>9/14</u>___ Time ___<u>3:15</u>___ A.M. ☐ P.M. ☒
WHILE YOU WERE OUT
☐ Mr./ ☐ Ms./ ☐ Mrs. _____
Phone _____
    Area code   Number   Extension
☐ telephoned   ☐ please call
☐ returned your call   ☐ will call back
Message: _____
_____

10 Label the pictures.

1.

2.

3.

4.

5.

11 Look at the pictures. Then complete the conversations.

1. **A:** Guest services. May I help you?

   B: Yes, please. Could you bring up some _____?
   1.

   A: Certainly.

   B: And I could use a _____, too. My hair is wet,
   2.
   and I don't see one in the bathroom.

   A: Sure. We'll bring those up right away. Anything else?

   B: Oh, yes. I have a lot of dirty clothes. Could someone

   please _____?
   3.

   A: Yes, of course.

   B: I think that's all. Thanks!

2. **A:** Front Desk. May I help you?

   B: Yes, I'd like to go for a swim. Is the _____ still open?
   4.

   A: No, I'm sorry, it closed at 9:00.

   B: Oh. Well, maybe a workout. How about the _____?
   5.

   A: No, it also just closed.

   B: Oh, no. Well, I guess I'll have to do some work then.

   Is the _____ still open?
   6.

   A: No, I'm sorry, it closed at 6:30. But you do have high-speed
   Internet access in your room.

   B: Oh, OK. Thanks.

12

Extra reading comprehension

Read *Where to Stay in New York* on page 34 of the Student's Book again.
Then read the statements and check <u>true</u>, <u>false</u>, or <u>no information</u>.

	true	false	no information
1. The Plaza is the most expensive hotel.	☐	☐	☐
2. The Casablanca Hotel is in the Theater District.	☐	☐	☐
3. The Hotel Chelsea has suites.	☐	☐	☐
4. The Peninsula is a budget hotel.	☐	☐	☐
5. The Broadway Inn is noisy.	☐	☐	☐
6. The Habitat Hotel is pet friendly.	☐	☐	☐

13 Read the travel guide about places to stay in Dublin, Ireland.

SLEEPING IN DUBLIN

€€€ Very expensive / €€ Moderately priced / € Budget

The Shelbourne Hotel

€€€ *History, Location*
Built in 1824, the Shelbourne is the most famous hotel in Dublin and a home-away-from-home for generations of politicians, writers, and actors. In fact, in 1922 the Irish Constitution was written in Room 112! Overlooking Saint Stephen's Green public park in the heart of Dublin, the location is perfect for sightseeing and shopping. Even if you don't stay here, you must go for afternoon tea in the elegant Lord Mayor's Lounge.

restaurant, room service, laundry service, business center, Internet service

The Morgan Hotel

€€€ *Style, Nightlife*
If you're crazy about style, the Morgan Hotel is your place. With very modern décor and designer furniture, this chic hotel is a favorite of people who work in fashion and music. The Morgan is located in the trendy Temple Bar district—an area popular with young people and *the* center of nightlife in Dublin. Note: Can be noisy at night.

restaurant, room service, laundry service, business center, Internet service, fitness room

The Aberdeen Lodge

€€ *Atmosphere, Service*
A short train ride from the Dublin city center, in a neighborhood of beautiful old homes and gardens, the Aberdeen Lodge is the perfect place for a quiet and relaxing stay. The friendly staff welcomes guests with tea and cookies and is very helpful with tourist advice. Suites feature working fireplaces. Don't miss breakfast in the lovely dining room overlooking the garden. Note: There is no elevator.

restaurant, room service, laundry service

The Camden Court

€€ *Convenience, Location*
The Camden Court is a large hotel that offers business travelers a good night's sleep and lot of amenities at an affordable price. Rooms are small but clean and comfortable. A short walk from Saint Stephen's Green, the location is perfect—close to tourist attractions, restaurants, and shopping. The Camden Court is a good choice for business or pleasure.

pool, sauna, fitness room, room service, business center, free Internet service, beauty salon, restaurant, free parking

Trinity College

€ *Price, Location*
Experience student life—without the exams!—at this beautiful, historic university located in the center of Dublin. From June to September, visitors can reserve single and double rooms while students are away for the summer holiday. Rooms are large and clean, but don't expect many amenities or services. Not all rooms have their own bathrooms.

cafeteria-style restaurant, free breakfast

SOURCE: *Lonely Planet Dublin City Guide*

14 Complete the chart. Use the travel guide in Exercise 13 to list an advantage and a disadvantage of each hotel.

Hotel	Advantage	Disadvantage
The Shelbourne Hotel		
The Morgan Hotel		
The Aberdeen Lodge		
The Camden Court		
Trinity College		

15 Read about the people's hotel needs and preferences. Use the travel guide in Exercise 13 to decide where the people should or shouldn't stay. Write statements with <u>had better (not)</u> or <u>should (not)</u>.

I want to meet other people my age and walk to clubs at night.

1. _____

_____

Peter broke his leg, but we can't change our flight. We need to be close to the sights and comfortable.

2. _____

_____

I'm traveling in the summer. Location is important to me, but I'm on a budget.

3. _____

_____

I'm attending a conference in Dublin. I'll have to wake up early, so I'd like someplace quiet. Oh, and I've got to be able to exercise.

4. _____

_____

GRAMMAR BOOSTER

A Write sentences. Use <u>have to</u>, <u>must not</u>, <u>don't have to</u>, or <u>doesn't have to</u>.

1. Employees and guests / smoke in the hotel _____

2. Hotel guests / check out before noon _____

3. A guest / use anything from the minibar _____

4. Hotel maids / make up the rooms _____

5. Hotel guests / reuse their towels, but they can _____

6. We / forget to unplug the iron _____

B Read the situation. Write a suggestion. Use <u>could</u>, <u>should</u>, <u>ought to</u>, <u>shouldn't</u>, <u>had better</u>, or <u>had better not</u>.

1. The 7:00 show is sold out. _____

2. We have a lot of luggage. _____

3. It's expensive to take a taxi to the airport. _____

4. The play starts at 8:00. _____

5. The Peninsula Hotel is very expensive. _____

6. We don't know where to go for dinner. _____

C Write a rule for each place. Use <u>be supposed to</u> or <u>not supposed to</u>.

1. a hospital: _*You're not supposed to use your cell phone in a hospital.*_

2. a restaurant: _____

3. a movie theater: _____

4. an airplane: _____

5. a museum: _____

6. the library: _____

D Complete the conversation using <u>will</u> or <u>won't</u>. Use contractions when possible.

A: _____ you be staying with us
    1.
   another night?

B: No, we _____ . But I think we
            2.
   _____ be back next month.
     3.

A: Great. How _____ you be paying today?
             4.

B: I _____ use my credit card, if that's OK.
    5.

A: Sure. That _____ be fine.
          6.

E Look at the pictures. What do you think the man is going to do?
Write sentences with a form of <u>be going to</u> or <u>not be going to</u>.

1. _____   2. _____   3. _____

_____   _____   _____

4. _____   5. _____

_____   _____

F Complete the conversations. Use the correct form of <u>be going to</u> if there is a plan
for the future or <u>will</u> if there is not a plan.

1. **A:** Have you decided about your vacation yet?

   B: Yes, we have. We _____ to India!

1. go

   A: Wow! When _____ you _____ ?

2. leave

   B: We _____ out on the 20th.

3. fly

   A: That's fantastic. Where _____ you _____?

4. stay

   B: I don't know yet. I guess we should make hotel reservations—or maybe

   we _____ just _____ something when we arrive.

5. find

2. **A:** Guess what? I _____ into a new apartment next week.

6. move

   B: That's great news! I _____ you if you like. What day _____

7. help

   you _____?

8. move

   A: Thanks! It's this Saturday at 9 A.M. OK?

   B: Oh, no! I _____ my sister at the airport then.

9. pick up

   A: No problem. Just come by when you're free.

A Read the hotel reviews in Exercise 13 on page 22 again. Complete each statement with a reason, according to the information in the reviews. Write the letter on the line.

1. _____ I prefer the Shelbourne . . .

2. _____ I'm going to stay at the Morgan . . .

3. _____ I'd like to stay at the Aberdeen Lodge . . .

4. _____ I'd rather stay at the Camden Court . . .

5. _____ I chose Trinity College . . .

a. because I'm not that big on noisy cities.

b. since I'm looking for the cheapest accommodations.

c. because I'm interested in Irish history.

d. since I want to be in Temple Bar.

e. since I'm going to rent a car.

B Rewrite the sentences in Exercise A, placing the dependent clause at the beginning of each sentence. Use a comma.

1. _____

2. _____

3. _____

4. _____

5. _____

C Look at the hotel reviews in Exercise 13. Which hotel would you rather stay at? Write the name of the hotel in the circle. List reasons with <u>because</u> or <u>since</u> in the boxes.

because

since

because

since

D On a separate sheet of paper, write a paragraph about the hotel you chose in Exercise C. Explain why you would like to stay there. Give reasons, using <u>because</u> or <u>since</u>. Are there any disadvantages? After you write your paragraph, check carefully to make sure that there are no sentence fragments.

Cars and Driving

1 Complete each sentence with a car type from the box.

a convertible	a minivan	an SUV	a luxury car	a compact car

1. Mavis loves hiking. She has _____ with four-wheel drive that she can drive on rough roads when she takes a trip to the mountains.

2. If you just need a car that's small and easy to park, _____ would be great for you.

3. Mrs. Jeter drives _____ to take her husband to work and their five children to school every morning.

4. Peter thinks that owning _____ is really cool. He said, "You can have the roof down and enjoy the sun, wind, and beautiful sky when the weather is nice."

5. Jack is the president of a big company and he drives _____ with expensive leather seats.

2 Read the phone conversation. Then complete the rental form.

Agent: Good afternoon. L & M Car Rental. How can I help you?

Renter: Hello. I'd like to make a reservation for June 10th.

Agent: Certainly. What type of car do you need?

Renter: A compact car.

Agent: Let's see . . . I'm afraid I don't have a compact available for that date. Is a full-size sedan OK?

Renter: That's fine.

Agent: How long do you need the car for?

Renter: For eight days. Can I pick up the car here in Middletown and return it at Bradley Airport?

Agent: Yes, that's fine. But there is a drop-off fee for one-way rentals.

Renter: All right. One last question: where are you located?

Agent: We're at 355 South Street in Middletown.

L & M Car Rental Agency, Ltd.

Pick up date: _____
Pick up location: _____
Drop off date: _____
Drop off location: _____

Choose the correct response. Circle the letter.

1. "How may I help you?"
   a. I have a reservation.   b. Just a moment.   c. That's right.

2. "The name is Suman Patel."
   a. We were expecting you.   b. You're all set.   c. That's all ready to go.

3. "Do you need a wagon or a minivan?"
   a. That's correct.   b. Certainly, sir.   c. Either way.

4. "Could I see your driver's license?"
   a. Here you go.   b. No, I don't.   c. Here are the keys.

5. "I have you picking up the car on April 12th."
   a. I don't have it with me.   b. That's correct.   c. Either way.

LESSON 1

4   **Label the car parts.**

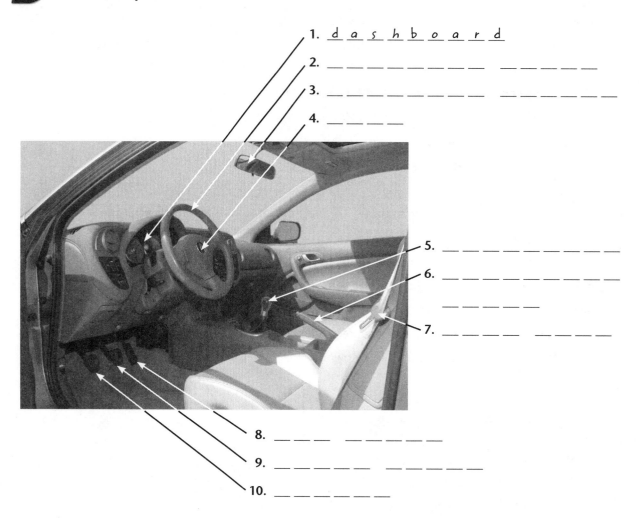

1. d a s h b o a r d
2. ___ ___ ___ ___ ___ ___ ___   ___ ___ ___ ___ ___
3. ___ ___ ___ ___ ___ ___ ___ ___   ___ ___ ___ ___ ___
4. ___ ___ ___ ___ ___

5. ___ ___ ___ ___ ___ ___ ___ ___ ___
6. ___ ___ ___ ___ ___ ___ ___ ___
   ___ ___ ___ ___ ___
7. ___ ___ ___ ___   ___ ___ ___

8. ___ ___ ___   ___ ___ ___ ___ ___
9. ___ ___ ___ ___ ___   ___ ___ ___ ___
10. ___ ___ ___ ___ ___ ___

5 Complete the conversation with the past continuous or the simple past tense.

A: Hi, Sandra. What's wrong?

B: I _____ an accident on the way home today.
   1. have

A: Oh, no! How _____ it _____?
   2. happen

B: Well, I _____ home when my sister
   3. drive

_____. She _____
4. call   5. ask

what I _____, and I _____
           6. do   7. tell

her I _____ home and would see
         8. go

her soon. But she _____ she had a funny
                        9. say

story that she just <u>had</u> to tell me. Anyway, by the end of the

story, I _____ so hard I couldn't see—and
         10. laugh

I _____ right into a stop sign.
   11. drive

6 Choose the correct response. Write the letter on the line.

1. "I had an accident today." _____

2. "Are you OK?" _____

3. "How did it happen?" _____

4. "Luckily, I was wearing my seat belt." _____

5. "Was there much damage?" _____

a. The other driver was speeding.

b. Not really. The other driver will have to replace a taillight.

c. Thank goodness.

d. Yes, I'm fine. No one was hurt.

e. How awful.

7 CHALLENGE. Have you or has someone you know ever had an accident? What happened? Write a note to a friend about it.

8 Look at the pictures. Write the letter of the correct picture after each phrasal verb.

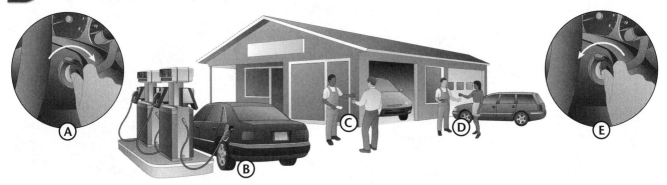

1. fill up _____   2. turn on _____   3. drop off _____   4. turn off _____   5. pick up _____

9 CHALLENGE. Complete the note below. Use the correct phrasal verb from Exercise 8. Sometimes you will need to use direct object pronouns.

> Hi, Lisa!
>
> I made an appointment to have Stan fix the car today. Can you _____
> 1.
> at the service station this afternoon? Tell Stan that the left turn signal isn't working.
> This morning I could _____ , but now it's stuck, and I can't seem to
> 2.
> _____ . Ask him to call me when the car is done. I'll _____
> 3.   4.
> on my way home from work.
>
> Love, Daniel
>
> P.S. While you're there, could you _____ the tank? See you tonight!
> 5.

10 Choose the correct response. Circle the letter.

1. "I'm dropping off my rental car."
   a. It's all ready to go.   b. Was everything OK?   c. Was there much damage?

2. "Any problems?"
   a. I just filled it up.   b. The sunroof won't open.   c. I'm sorry to hear that.

3. "What's wrong with the air conditioning?"
   a. It won't close.   b. It's out of gas.   c. It's making a funny sound.

4. "Is the gas tank full?"
   a. No. That's it.   b. Oh, no! I forgot to fill it up.   c. I wasn't paying attention.

11 **Read the ads for the three cars. Then choose the best answer to each question, according to the ads. Circle the letter.**

RAMUNO

The Ramuno is really inexpensive, and you'll find it easier than ever to own one today. You can start saving money because it's good on gas. You can even save time parking when you drive a Ramuno—with the Ramuno's size, you'll never have to worry if you can only find a tight parking spot.

RAMUNO

Love outdoor adventures? Feel the power of the four-wheel drive Vicic. It'll take you just about anywhere. The new design allows you to enjoy a comfortable ride even on the toughest mountain roads. Come test-drive it today!

VICIC

Zatec You'll be amazed by how the Zatec provides comfortable seating for nine people and still has plenty of cargo room. Whether it's a few suitcases for your family's road trip or all the bags from a long day's shopping at the mall, you won't have any problem fitting them all in.

1. Which of the three cars can take the most passengers?
   a. the Vicic   b. the Zatec   c. the Ramuno

2. What type of car do you think the Zatec is?
   a. a sports car   b. a full-size sedan   c. a van

3. Which of the three cars is most likely a compact car?
   a. the Ramuno   b. the Vicic   c. the Zatec

12 **Read about the people. Which of the three cars in Exercise 11 is best for each person? Explain your reasons.**

1. Bryan is planning a cross-country road trip with his girlfriend. They want to do a lot of sightseeing in the countryside and go hiking in the mountains.

   _____

   _____

2. Rachel has four kids and she works part-time. She has a lot of driving to do for work, the kids, and shopping. And she needs to carry a lot of things around.

   _____

   _____

3. Danny recently graduated from college and has just started working. He doesn't have a lot of money. He's single and lives by himself. His office is on a busy street downtown, far away from where he lives. He plans to drive to work.

   _____

   _____

13

Extra reading comprehension

Read *Six Tips For Defensive Driving* on page 46 of the Student's Book again. Then read the statements and write <u>D</u> for defensive driving, <u>A</u> for aggressive driving, or <u>I</u> for inattentive driving.

1. _____ tailgating to make others go faster

2. _____ following the "3-second rule"

3. _____ multitasking while driving

4. _____ checking your mirrors frequently

5. _____ slowing down in bad weather

6. _____ pulling over to avoid a bad driver

7. _____ cutting other drivers off

8. _____ talking on the phone while driving

14 Read the article about renting a car in the U.S.

Driving in the U.S.A.

Planning a trip to the U.S.? Have you thought about how you'll get around? If you're going to stay in a big city such as New York, Chicago, or San Francisco, public transportation is the most convenient option. However, to travel almost anywhere else in the U.S., you'll need a car.

Car Rental Tips

Requirements: Most car rental agencies require drivers to be at least 25 years old. Some allow younger drivers but may charge a higher rate. To rent a car in the U.S., you will need a credit card and driver's license. Visitors can usually rent a car and drive with a driver's license from their home country. However, if your license is in a language that doesn't use the Roman alphabet, you should obtain an International Driving Permit in English.

Cost: Car rental rates change often, and you can usually save money by shopping around for the best price. Be sure to check travel and rental agency websites for special sales and discounts. Look for package deals that offer car rental and airfare or hotel for one low price. If your schedule is flexible, compare prices for different travel dates. It is often cheaper to rent a car on weekends or for a full week rather than a few days.

Hidden charges: Always read the small print on your car rental agreement carefully—to check for hidden

charges such as taxes, airport surcharges, and drop-off fees (an extra charge for returning a car to a different location from where you picked up). Make sure that you drop off the car with a full tank of gas. Rental agencies charge a fill-up fee and high gas prices if they have to fill up the gas tank.

Safety: Before you leave the car rental lot, inspect the car carefully for damage and make sure everything is working properly. Ask the agent to note any problems on the rental form. Take a few minutes to become familiar with the car. Adjust your seat and mirrors. Locate the controls for the lights, turn signals, and windshield wipers. Then, buckle up! Wear your seat belt, and ask your passengers to wear theirs, too. Most states have seat belt laws, and all states require that young children and babies sit in the back seat in special child seats. When you're ready, follow the traffic laws for the states you'll be driving in. If you're not sure, check with car rental staff before you hit the road.

Sources: usatourist.com, novacarhire.com

15 Find and circle the phrases in the article in Exercise 14. Then match the phrases and their meanings. Write the letter on the line.

1. _____ get around

2. _____ package deals

3. _____ hidden charges

4. _____ fill-up fee

5. _____ buckle up

6. _____ hit the road

a. extra costs that are not clearly stated

b. fasten your seat belt

c. travel from place to place

d. begin a car trip

e. specials that offer two or more services for one price

f. an extra charge for returning a car without a full tank of gas

16 Answer the questions about renting a car in the U.S. Use information from the article in Exercise 14. Explain your answers.

1. I am 23 years old. Can I rent a car? _____
   _____

2. Do I need an International Driving Permit to drive in the U.S.? _____
   _____

3. Where can I get the best price for a car rental? _____
   _____

4. I want to pick up a car in New York and drop it off at Los Angeles International Airport. What hidden charges should I check for? _____
   _____

5. We are traveling with small children. Are there any special requirements? _____
   _____

GRAMMAR BOOSTER

A Complete each sentence in your own way. Use the past continuous or the simple past tense.

1. They were having dinner when _____.
2. While _____ , it started to rain.
3. While Marie was watching TV, her husband _____.
4. When _____ , I was leaving my office.
5. He had an accident while _____.

B CHALLENGE. Look at the pictures. On a separate sheet of paper, write a story about what happened using the words and phrases in the boxes.

drive	run in front of	hit
talk on cell phone	stop	hurt
not pay attention		damage

C Put the words in order and write sentences. If a sentence can be written in two ways, write it both ways.

1. dropped / Margo / off / the car

   Margo dropped off the car. OR Margo dropped the car off.

2. up / it / Sam / picked

   _____

3. the tank / filled / I / up

   _____

4. can't / turn / on / Sue / the headlights

   _____

5. turn / off / I / can't / them

   _____

6. like / He'd / it / to / drop / off / at noon

   _____

7. I / to / need / up / it / fill

   _____

8. picked / the car / William / up / has

   _____
   _____

D Label each underlined noun either <u>common</u> or <u>proper</u>. Then rewrite each sentence, replacing the underlined noun with a subject or object pronoun.

1. _common_
   <u>The car door</u> is making a funny sound.

   It is making a funny sound.

2. <u>Mr. Lee</u> rented the convertible.

   _____

3. The mechanic replaced <u>the taillight</u>.

   _____

4. Alex already called <u>Econo-Car</u>.

   _____

5. <u>The Amigo minivan</u> hit the tree.

   _____

6. My sister will drop off <u>the keys</u>.

   _____

7. Mrs. Lane is going to pick up <u>her son</u> at 5:00.

   _____
   _____

A **Insert commas where necessary in the following sentences.**

1. You need a driver's license and a credit card to rent a car.

2. The car rental charge included a drop-off fee a fill-up fee and an airport surcharge.

3. You should shop around for the best price and make a reservation.

4. Adjust your seat mirrors and the radio.

5. Locate the controls for the lights and turn signals.

B **Combine each pair of sentences into one sentence consisting of two independent clauses. Use _and_.**

1. The driver wasn't paying attention. He hit the car in front of him.

   _____

2. It's raining. The sunroof won't close.

   _____

3. Lucy has five kids. She drives a minivan.

   _____

4. The GPS isn't working. We're lost.

   _____

C **Complete the statements. Look back at the article in Exercise 14 for ideas. Add commas.**

1. Many areas of the U.S. don't have good public transportation. Therefore _____

   _____.

2. Car rental rates change frequently. Therefore _____

   _____.

3. To find a good rate, check travel and car rental agency websites. In addition _____

   _____.

4. Return your rental car with a full tank of gas. If you don't, you'll pay double the regular price for gas.

   In addition _____

   _____.

5. Most states have seat belt laws. Therefore _____

   _____.

6. Small children must sit in the back seat. In addition _____

   _____.

D **On a separate sheet of paper, write about your driving or a friend or family member's driving. Include good and bad driving behaviors.**

1 **Complete the sentences with salon services.**

1. Your fingernails look great. Did you get a __ __⟨__⟩__ __ __ __ __?

2. His hair was getting long, so he made an appointment for a __⟨__⟩__ __ __ __ __.

3. I have a lot of tension in my shoulders from sitting at the computer. I need a __ __ __⟨__⟩__ __ __.

4. After my __ __ __ __ __⟨__⟩, my skin felt smooth and soft.

5. I don't need a __ __ __ __ __⟨__⟩. I just washed my hair.

Now unscramble the circled letters. What's the word? _____

2 **Complete the conversation with questions from the box. Write the letter.**

> **a.** Do you think I could get a massage, too?
>
> **b.** Is it customary to leave a tip?
>
> **c.** How long will I have to wait?
>
> **d.** Would it be possible to get a facial?
>
> **e.** Can I charge it to my room?

Client: _____? I don't have an appointment.
　　　　　1.

Receptionist: You're in luck. A client just canceled his appointment.

Client: Great. _____?
　　　　　　　2.

Receptionist: Yes. But you might have to wait a bit.

Client: _____?
　　　　　3.

Receptionist: Let's see. I have something at 4:00.

Client: That's fine. _____?
　　　　　　　　　4.

Receptionist: Certainly. Just sign here, please. Then I'll show you to the dressing area.

Client: I have one more question. _____?
　　　　　　　　　　　　　　　　5.

Receptionist: That's up to you. But most clients give about 10 percent.

3 How often do you get these salon services? Look at each picture and write a sentence.

1. _____

2. _____

3. _____

4. _____

5. _____

LESSON 1

4 Complete the word webs. Write personal care products on the lines.

1 Tooth care

2 Nail care

3 Hair care

4 Skin care

5 Shaving

6 Makeup

5 Complete the sentences. Circle the correct words.

1. This store doesn't have (much / many) combs.
2. I can't find (some / any) sunscreen, but here's (some / any) body lotion.
3. Do you have (much / a lot of) razors at home?
4. She doesn't have (much / many) hair spray left.
5. Emma needs (some / any) dental floss.
6. Helen doesn't need (some / much) soap.
7. Do you have (any / many) deodorant?
8. I have (some / any) extra shampoo.
9. I found shaving cream, but there aren't (some / any) razors here.
10. Are you out of toothpaste? I have (some / much).

LESSON 2

6 Complete each statement or question with <u>someone</u>, <u>no one</u>, or <u>anyone</u>. In some cases, more than one answer is correct.

1. _____ made a ten o'clock appointment for a pedicure.
2. Excuse me. _____ is at the front desk. Can _____ help me?
3. I'm sorry. We don't have _____ available to help you now.
4. There's _____ ahead of you. Do you mind waiting?
5. Did you see _____ you know at the hair salon?
6. There's _____ waiting for a massage.

7 Look at the pictures. Write statements using the words in parentheses and <u>someone</u>, <u>no one</u>, or <u>anyone</u>. In some cases, more than one answer is correct.

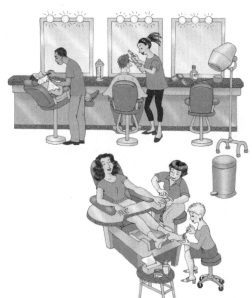

1. (get / shave) *There's someone getting a shave.*
2. (give / facial) _____
3. (get / haircut) _____
4. (use / comb) _____
5. (give / massage) _____
6. (use / shampoo) _____
7. (get / manicure / pedicure) _____
8. (use / nail file) _____

8

Extra reading comprehension

Read the article *Cosmetic surgery—for everyone?* on page 56 of the Student's Book again. Then match the terms with their definitions.

1. _____ chocoholic

2. _____ liposuction

3. _____ hair restoration

4. _____ depilatory

5. _____ face-lift

6. _____ chemical peel

a. a cream that removes unwanted hair on the body

b. surgery to correct baldness

c. someone who likes chocolate very much and eats it all the time

d. surgery to remove wrinkles and other signs of aging from the face

e. treatment for wrinkles that removes the top layer of skin on the face

f. surgery to remove fat from the body

9   **Read the article about ways to improve personal appearance.**

Look Great — Without Cosmetic Surgery

Want to lose weight? Look younger? More and more people are turning to cosmetic surgery. While liposuction or a face-lift might sound like an easy way to get the results you want, it's important to remember that cosmetic surgery is, in fact, surgery. And surgery is not easy. It's expensive, painful, and potentially dangerous. So, before you go under the knife, give these safe, low-cost ways to improve your appearance a try.

1. Get enough sleep. It's called "beauty sleep" for a reason. Nighttime is when your skin and hair cells renew and repair themselves. Also, more blood flows to your skin when you're sleeping, making it brighter. Most people know that lack of sleep can cause dark circles under your eyes. But many don't realize that not getting eight hours of sleep a night can also lead to wrinkles and weight gain.

2. Drink a lot of water. Get into the habit of drinking more water. Well-hydrated skin is less likely to develop blemishes or wrinkles. For clearer, smoother skin, try to drink at least eight glasses of water a day. The more water.you drink, the better your skin will look. Also, drinking water throughout the day will curb your appetite—making it easier to eat less and lose weight.

3. Exercise regularly. The physical benefits of exercise include reduced body fat and more toned muscles. While 60 minutes of daily vigorous exercise is ideal, begin with a reasonable goal—maybe 30 minutes three times a week. Choose something you enjoy, and enroll in a class, join a team, or make plans to workout regularly with a group of friends.

4. Eat a healthy diet. To lose weight, you need to change your eating habits. You should choose foods that are low in fat and low in calories. You probably knew that already, but did you know that some foods can also improve the appearance of your skin and hair? For beautiful skin, eat foods rich in antioxidants. Darkly colored fruits and vegetables contain antioxidants, which help repair sun damage and prevent wrinkles. Blueberries, spinach, and carrots have a lot of antioxidants. For shiny, healthy hair, eat foods high in lean protein like fish, beans, and nuts. These foods may also help prevent hair loss.

What's good for your health is also good for your looks. So, get a good night's sleep and some exercise. Drink lots of water and eat fresh, natural foods—mostly fruits and veggies. It costs almost nothing and doesn't hurt, so what have you got to lose? Except maybe a few kilos!

Source: ehow.com

10 Complete the chart. Use information from the article in Exercise 9. How much sleep, water, and exercise does the article recommend? What types of foods does it suggest?

	What the article recommends
sleep	
water	
exercise	
diet	

11 What are the results of doing what the article recommends?

| sleep | |

| water | |

| exercise | |

| diet | |

12 CHALLENGE. How much sleep and exercise do you get? How much water do you drink? What types of foods do you eat? After reading the article, what would you like to do differently? Why?

13 Think of a famous person or someone you know that represents both inner and outer beauty. Describe the person's inner qualities on the lines inside the head. Describe the person's physical features on the lines outside the head.

Name of person: _____

14 Complete the statements with words from the box.

attractive	health	heart	inner
kindness	modest	outer	patient

1. Someone who is a good listener and lets others speak is _____.

2. Beautiful skin and hair and a nice body are features of _____ beauty.

3. Goodness, _____ to other people, truthfulness, and happiness with life are qualities of _____ beauty.

4. Someone who has nice physical features is _____.

5. The condition of a person's body is called _____.

6. Someone who doesn't talk proudly about his or her own appearance or abilities is _____.

7. "The best and most beautiful things in the world cannot be seen, nor touched . . . but are felt in the _____." –Helen Keller

A Look in the medicine cabinet. Write sentences about the products you see, using words from the box.

bar	bottle	can	package	tube

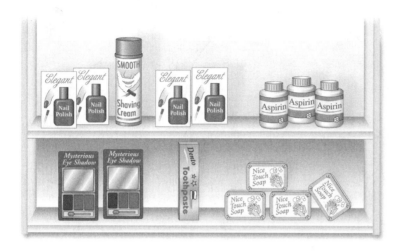

1. _____There are four bottles of nail polish._____

2. _____

3. _____

4. _____

5. _____

6. _____

B Answer the questions about your own personal care products. Write complete sentences with <u>some</u> or <u>any</u>.

1. Do you have any dental floss at home?

_____

2. Do you need some toothpaste from the store?

_____

3. Is there any shaving cream in your bathroom?

_____

4. Are you wearing any perfume or aftershave now?

_____

5. Do you have some sunscreen at home?

_____

6. Is there any makeup in your bathroom?

_____

7. Would you like some hand lotion?

_____

C Write a ✔ next to the sentences that are correct.

1. ☐ a. There isn't enough soap.
   ☐ b. There isn't too many soap.

2. ☐ a. Do you have too much razors?
   ☐ b. Do you have too many razors?

3. ☐ a. I don't have too many makeup.
   ☐ b. I don't have enough makeup.

4. ☐ a. Does she have too many toothpaste?
   ☐ b. Does she have enough toothpaste?

5. ☐ a. There isn't too much shampoo.
   ☐ b. There isn't too many shampoo.

D Complete each sentence with <u>too much</u>, <u>too many</u>, or <u>enough</u>.

1. I couldn't wash my hair. There wasn't _____ shampoo left.

2. I'm going to the store. Do you have _____ flour to make the cake?

3. There are just _____ people here. I don't feel like waiting.

4. Don't you think that's _____ money for a pedicure? It's too expensive.

5. You bought _____ nail files. We only need one.

E Complete each sentence with <u>fewer</u> or <u>less</u>.

1. Bridget should wear _____ makeup. She looks beautiful without it!

2. Budget hotels have _____ amenities than expensive hotels.

3. This film has _____ violence than that new action adventure movie.

4. The compact car will use _____ gas than the SUV.

5. Which ticket line has _____ people waiting in it?

6. The rental agency has _____ cars with manual transmission than with automatic transmission.

F Complete each sentence with <u>something</u> or <u>anything</u>.

1. We have _____ new at our salon.

2. He didn't take _____ for his headache.

3. Do you need _____ from the drugstore?

4. I didn't see _____ I like in the catalog.

5. I always buy _____ from that store.

6. I just can't relax. There is always _____ to do.

7. They gave me _____ to drink at the salon.

8. I don't know _____ about cosmetic surgery.

G Read the paragraph. Find and correct five mistakes.

> I went to the supermarket today because I needed to get nothing to cook for my dinner party tonight. I wanted to buy some juice, too. But when I got there, there wasn't nothing on the shelf! I went to the store manager and asked him why the shelves were empty. He apologized and said there was anything wrong with the delivery truck. "It didn't come today," he told me. He said I'd have to wait until the next day. Now I don't have something to serve for the big party tonight. I've never seen nothing like this!

WRITING BOOSTER

A Think about a time when you had bad service at a place of business such as a salon, a car rental agency, a hotel, a movie theater, or a restaurant. Write an e-mail message to the manager complaining about the service. Describe the problem you had. Suggest a way for the business to improve.

To:	
Subject:	

B Prepare to turn your e-mail message into a formal business letter. Write the following information.

1. your address: _____

2. recipient's name and / or position and address:

   _____

3. today's date: _____

4. a salutation: _____

5. a complimentary close: _____

6. your signature and printed name: _____

C Now type (or write) your formal business letter. Use the e-mail message you wrote in Exercise A as the body of your letter. Include all the information from Exercise B.

Eating Well

1 Look at the Healthy Eating Pyramid. Then read the statements. Check <u>true</u> or <u>false</u>.

fats, oils, sweets
(rarely)

meat, fish, beans
2–3 servings per day for protein and vitamins

dairy
2–3 servings per day for calcium

fruit
2–4 servings per day for vitamins and fiber

vegetables
3–5 servings per day for vitamins and fiber

bread, grains, pasta
6–11 servings per day for carbohydrates

daily exercise and weight control

	true	false
1. The healthiest foods are at the top of the pyramid.	☐	☐
2. You should eat more vegetables than fish.	☐	☐
3. You should avoid breads and grains.	☐	☐
4. Dairy products are a good source of fiber.	☐	☐
5. You should eat fruit for carbohydrates.	☐	☐
6. Exercise is an important part of a healthy life.	☐	☐

2 Rewrite the false statements in Exercise 1 to make them true.

3 Complete the statements with phrases from the box.

I'd better pass	I have no idea	I'm watching my weight
I have to admit	I couldn't resist	

1. I'm on a low-fat diet because _____.

2. The pasta looks delicious, but _____. I'm on the Atkins diet.

3. I usually avoid animal products, but _____ the ice cream they served for dessert. I just had to have it!

4. _____ how much fat is in this cheeseburger—and I don't want to know. I just want to enjoy it!

5. Eating a low-fat, high-fiber diet hasn't been easy, but _____ I look and feel better as a result.

LESSON 1

4 Look at the pictures. What do you think the people are saying? Write sentences about the people and their food passions. Use the words and phrases from the box.

addict	big _____ eater	can't stand	~~crazy about~~	don't care for	love

1. I'm crazy about asparagus.

2. _____

3. _____

4. _____

5. _____

6. _____

5 **Read about Kate's food passions. Then complete each sentence with <u>used to</u> or <u>didn't use to</u> and the verb.**

When I was a kid, I loved sweets. I think I ate about five cookies a day! When I was a teenager, I started eating a lot of meat. I had steaks and fries almost every day. I didn't care for vegetables or fruit. Then on my 20th birthday, I decided I needed a change, so I became a vegetarian. These days I eat meat again, but I avoid fatty foods and sugar. I've lost a lot of weight and I feel much better.

Kate

1. Kate _____ a lot of sweets, but now she avoids sugar.
   eat

2. When she was a teenager, she _____ fatty foods.
   have

3. Before she turned 20, she _____ vegetables.
   like

4. She _____ a vegetarian, but now she eats meat.
   be

5. Kate _____ care of herself, but now she eats well.
   take

LESSON 2

6 **Choose the correct response. Write the letter on the line.**

1. _____ "Please help yourself."

2. _____ "I'll pass on the chocolates."

3. _____ "Don't you eat chicken?"

4. _____ "I'm sorry. I didn't know you were on a diet."

5. _____ "I'm a coffee addict. What about you?"

a. Actually, I've been cutting back.

b. Thanks. Everything smells so good.

c. It's not a problem.

d. Don't you eat sweets?

e. Actually, no. It's against my religion.

7 **Complete the statements with a food or drink to describe your own food preferences.**

1. I'm not crazy about _____.

2. I'm avoiding _____.

3. I don't care for _____.

4. I'm not much of a _____ drinker.

5. _____ doesn't / don't agree with me.

8 Complete the conversation with phrases from the box.

| is a vegetarian | is on a diet | is allergic to | doesn't care for | is avoiding |

A: Let's have a dinner party Friday night. Help me prepare the menu.

B: OK. Remember that my sister _____, so we can't make anything too fatty. Why don't you make some chicken?

A: I would, but Stella _____. She never eats meat. Maybe I can make that rice dish.

B: I don't know. Miguel is trying to eat healthy, whole-grain foods, so he _____ white rice these days.

A: OK . . . Then how about black bean soup with peppers?

B: Uh, I don't think Julio would like that. He _____ spicy food.

A: Is there anything that everyone can eat?

B: Hmm . . . I don't know, but I hope you'll make that delicious chocolate cake for dessert!

A: I can't. Don't you remember how sick Paul was at our last dinner? He _____ chocolate!

B: I've got an idea—why don't we just go out to eat? Then everyone can order what they want!

9 Complete each negative <u>yes</u> / <u>no</u> question.

1. **A:** *Didn't you go to Latvia* last year?
   B: Yes, I did. I went to Latvia in August.

2. **A:** _____ meat?
   B: No, I don't. I never touch meat.

3. **A:** _____ a doctor?
   B: No, she's not. David's mother is a dentist.

4. **A:** _____ a great play?
   B: Yes, it was terrific.

5. **A:** _____ more noodles?
   B: No, thanks. I'm full. I've had enough.

6. **A:** _____ China before?
   B: Actually, no. But I've been to Korea.

LESSON 3

10 Read the article on page 68 of the Student's Book again. Then complete the chart.

Extra reading comprehension

American eating habits	French eating habits
	consume rich food but stay thin
"clean their plates"	
	spend a long time at the table
drive to the supermarket	
	buy fresh food daily

11 Answer the questions with information from the article on page 68 of the Student's Book.

1. Why did Mireille Guiliano write her book *French Women Don't Get Fat*?

   _____

2. According to Guiliano, why don't French women get fat?

   _____

3. What lifestyle change has affected French eating habits recently?

   _____

12 Read the online article about making lifestyle changes.

How to make healthy lifestyle changes that last

If you've ever tried to change the way you eat or to lead a more active lifestyle, you know it isn't easy. Making a lifestyle change is challenging—and it's especially difficult to make changes that last. Often people try to make many big changes all at once without a clear idea of how they will accomplish their goals. They may struggle, get disappointed, and give up after a short period of time. Here are some tips to help you make healthy changes that become lifelong habits:

1 Make one change at a time. Replacing unhealthy behaviors with healthy ones takes time. If you try to change too much too fast, you won't be successful. Focus on one change you'd like to make. If your goal is to improve your eating habits, choose one thing to cut back on or add to your diet. Maybe resolve to stop drinking soda or eat some vegetables or fruit with every meal. When a new healthy behavior becomes part of your normal daily routine, you can take on another change.

2 Start small. Changes are often easier to make if they are small. Don't expect yourself to go from lying on the sofa watching TV every night to spending an hour a night at the gym. Instead, take "baby steps." For example, you could start by exercising twice a week for 30 minutes. Then, when you've done this successfully for a few weeks, try three times a week for 45 minutes.

3 Make a realistic plan. When you decide to make a lifestyle change, you need to plan what you will do and when, where, how often, etc. If more exercise is your goal, figure out how you will schedule it into your week and put it on your calendar. If you want to eat healthier, write down meals and snacks for the week. Keep the foods you'll need on hand, and consult your plan before you eat. Make sure the plan you create is achievable and that it works for your lifestyle. For example, if you're a big meat eater, a plan to eat only vegetables is not going to happen! Likewise, if you're not a morning person, don't plan daily workouts at 5:00 A.M.!

INFORMATION SOURCE: apa.com

3 Complete the statements with words and phrases from the box.

"baby step"	challenging	habits	realistic	struggle	successful

1. You want the changes you make to become _____—something you do regularly without thinking because you've done it so many times before.

2. It's difficult to make lifestyle changes. You may _____, but don't give up.

3. If you try to make many big changes all at once, you probably won't be _____.

4. If you want to stop drinking coffee, you could start by drinking two cups every morning instead of three. This is a _____.

5. When you plan to make a change, be _____. Set goals you can accomplish and that work for your lifestyle.

6. Trying to change the way you eat is _____. It takes a lot of effort.

4 Think about a lifestyle change you have tried to make. Was your change successful? On a separate sheet of paper, explain why or why not.

LESSON 4

15 Complete the postcard with the correct form of <u>taste</u>, <u>smell</u>, or <u>look</u>.

MARRAKECH

Hi Reiko,

I'm having a great time in Marrakech! Yesterday I walked in the main square, and it _____ like a scene from a movie!
1.
People in long, beautiful robes were everywhere, and there was so much food! I saw some fish that _____ like the kind we have
2.
at home. Somewhere else in the market, I couldn't see where, there was a kind of grilled meat that _____ terrific. I found it, but didn't know if I should try it.
3.
It _____ kind of strange, but I bought some anyway. It was delicious!
4.
It _____ both spicy and sweet. It wasn't at all what I expected!
5.
You should come here on your next vacation!

See you soon,
Junko

16 Complete the word webs. Write three examples of foods that match each adjective.

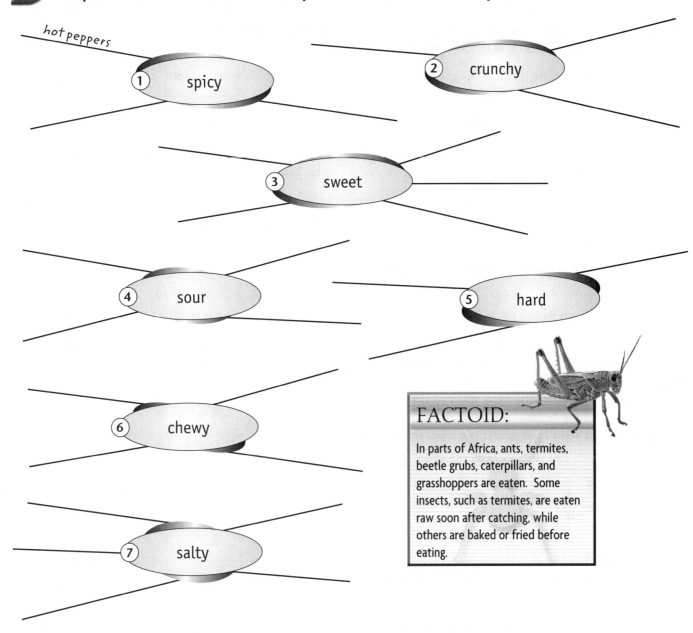

hot peppers

1 spicy

2 crunchy

3 sweet

4 sour

5 hard

6 chewy

7 salty

FACTOID:

In parts of Africa, ants, termites, beetle grubs, caterpillars, and grasshoppers are eaten. Some insects, such as termites, are eaten raw soon after catching, while others are baked or fried before eating.

17 Describe an unusual dish you have tried. Where and when did you eat it? What did it look, smell, and taste like? Would you recommend it to someone or not?

One of the strangest things I've ever eaten is . . .

GRAMMAR BOOSTER

A **Read the statements. Then write a sentence with <u>use to</u> or <u>used to</u> about a habitual action that is no longer true today.**

1. Since Charlie started going to the gym every day, he's lost so much weight.
   Charlie didn't use to go to the gym every day.

2. When he wasn't working, Scott made dinner every night. Now he doesn't have time.
   _____

3. Paul began getting up early every day when he had children.
   _____

4. As Cindy got older, her tastes changed. Now she actually likes vegetables.
   _____

5. I can't believe Judy doesn't eat meat anymore!
   _____

6. When Peter's doctor told him that he had better stop smoking, he quit.
   _____

7. After Pamela and Ed got married, they bought their first car.
   _____

B **Write a <u>yes</u> / <u>no</u> question for each response, using a form of <u>used to</u>.**

1. **A:** _Did you use to work in that part of the city?_
   B: Yes, I did. I used to work in that part of the city a few years ago.

2. **A:** _____
   B: No, they didn't. People didn't use to read the news online.

3. **A:** _____
   B: Yes, it did. Breakfast used to be free at the Windfield Inn.

4. **A:** _____
   B: No, they didn't. Foods didn't use to have labels.

5. **A:** _____
   B: Yes, I did. I used to live closer to work.

6. **A:** _____
   B: Yes, they did. Cars used to use a lot more gas.

7. **A:** _____
   B: No, I didn't. My brother used to drive a van, but not me.

C Complete the sentences with be used to, affirmative or negative.

1. Michelle has been on a low-fat, high-fiber diet for many years. She _____ fruits, vegetables, and whole grains. She _____ rich food, such as steak and ice cream.

2. Karen just got a haircut. It's very different from her old style. She _____ her new look yet.

3. We rented a minivan, but at home I drive a compact car. I _____ driving such a big car.

4. I _____ budget hotels, so it's a treat to stay in this expensive hotel with so many amenities.

5. Jeff is crazy about action movies. He _____ watching a lot of violence on the big screen.

D Complete the statements in your own way.

1. The Browns just moved from Alaska to Hawaii. They can't get used to _____
_____.

2. Rose recently moved from a small town to a big city. She's getting used to _____
_____.

3. Conor used to be a vegetarian. He still hasn't gotten used to _____.
_____.

Write three sentences about things you did often when you were a child. Use would.

When I was a child, I would play soccer all day on Saturdays.

1. _____
2. _____
3. _____

E Complete the conversations. Complete the negative yes / no questions and write short answers.

1. A: _____ you have any vegetarian friends?
   B: _____. None of my friends are vegetarian.

2. A: _____ you trying to lose weight?
   B: _____. I'm on a diet.

3. A: _____ he like spicy food?
   B: _____. He can't stand spicy food.

4. A: _____ there sardines on that pizza?
   B: _____. The pizza has sardines on it.

5. A: _____ Sandra allergic to fish?
   B: _____. She doesn't have any problem eating fish.

F Complete each conversation with a suggestion using <u>Why don't</u> or <u>Why doesn't</u>.

1. **A:** I'm too tired to cook dinner tonight.

   B: _____ go out to eat?

2. **A:** Mr. Lee's old van keeps breaking down.

   B: _____ buy a new car?

3. **A:** My mother thinks the hotel room will be too small.

   B: _____ reserve a suite?

4. **A:** That documentary was really long and boring!

   B: _____ watch a comedy next time?

WRITING BOOSTER

A Circle the best subordinating conjunction to complete each sentence.

1. It's important to eat fruits and vegetables (because / unless / although) they are a source of vitamins and fiber.

2. You should avoid fatty foods and sweets (unless / even though / if) you're watching your weight.

3. On the Atkins Diet, you can eat butter (since / even though / unless) it has a lot of fat.

4. You'll love the new Argentinean steakhouse El Matador (unless / if / because) you're a vegetarian.

5. (If / Since / Though) Hannah doesn't care for fish or seafood, we didn't go out for sushi.

6. (Because / If / Although) she's cutting back on sweets, Danielle had a piece of cake at the birthday party.

7. Kate is avoiding dairy products (even though / unless / because) they don't agree with her.

8. (Unless / If / Since) he has to stay up late studying, Andrew doesn't drink coffee.

9. (Although / If / Unless) children are taught to always "clean their plates," they may become overweight.

10. (Unless / Though / Because) it's difficult to change your habits, you can succeed by making one small change at a time.

B Think about your eating habits today and your eating habits when you were younger. Write six sentences: three about your eating habits now and three about how you used to eat. Use subordinating conjunctions.

1. _____

2. _____

3. _____

4. _____

5. _____

6. _____

C On a separate sheet of paper, write a paragraph about how your eating habits have changed.

About Personality

Preview

1 **Read each description. Then guess the color being described.**

1. People associate this color with power, intelligence, and sometimes evil. It's popular in fashion because it makes people look slimmer. _____

2. People associate this color with cleanliness and purity. It's popular in decorating because it goes with everything. _____

3. This is one of the most appealing colors. The color of the ocean and the sky, people find it peaceful and calming. It's a great color for a bedroom. It's not a good choice for a dining room—unless you're on a diet. _____

4. This color is associated with energy and excitement. It makes your heart beat faster—and increases your appetite. It's a popular color for fast cars and restaurants. In China, it means good luck. _____

2 **Read the Photo Story on page 75 of the Student's Book again. Match each phrase or statement with its meaning.**

1. _____ getting a little tired of

2. _____ to me it was

3. _____ pulling your leg

4. _____ Good point.

5. _____ I'd hate to have to

6. _____ on the wrong track

7. _____ goes with everything

a. in my opinion it was

b. That's true. I hadn't thought of that.

c. I don't want to

d. looks good with all things

e. bored with

f. not thinking correctly about this

g. joking by saying something that isn't true

3 **Write about your own color preferences.**

1. What's your favorite color? How does it make you feel?

_____

2. What room in your home would you like to paint a different color? What color would you choose? Why?

_____

3. Paint colors have names that describe specific shades—such as "tomato red" or "emerald green." Create a name for your favorite shade of your favorite color.

_____

> **FACTOID: Men, women, and colors**
>
> **Studies have found that women prefer red over blue, but men prefer blue over red.**

4 Complete Lucia's letter. Use gerunds and infinitives. Remember to put the verbs in the correct tense.

Hi Rebecca,

Well, I finally made a change! Last week I said to myself, "I _____ at our
1. can't stand / look

old kitchen walls one more day!" So I _____ them! My roommate Sara said
2. decide / repaint

we should _____ a plan before we do it. She even _____
3. discuss / make   4. suggest / take

a month or two to think about it. She said we should _____
5. practice / paint

first, but I already know how to paint. I don't _____. Anyway, I
6. need / learn

_____ new things. Finally, we _____ the kitchen a
7. not mind / try   8. choose / give

cheerful color—bright yellow! I'm not sure, but Sara _____ the new
9. not seem / like

color. In fact, I don't think she _____! But I hope she does, because I
10. enjoy / paint

_____ the living room next. I _____ it tomato red!
11. plan / paint   12. would like / paint

What do you think about that?

Lucia

5 Complete each sentence with a gerund or infinitive and an adjective from the box.

annoying	boring	depressing	enjoyable	exciting	relaxing

1. I've had the most stressful week at work! I need _____ a massage this weekend.
   get
   I find it so _____.

2. We don't want _____ tonight's game. Our favorite team is in the championship.
   miss
   It's going to be really _____!

3. Most kids hate _____ shopping. They think it's not any fun and complain, "This is
   go
   so _____."

4. I had to ask a classmate to please quit _____ his pencil on the desk. I found it very
   tap
   _____.

5. I don't feel like _____ that film. I hear it's very _____. I'm not in
   watch
   the mood for a sad movie.

6. Max usually doesn't mind _____. He finds it pretty _____.
   exercise

6 Write about your plans for the weekend. Use verbs with direct object infinitives, such as <u>need</u>, <u>plan</u>, <u>want</u>, and <u>would like</u>.

LESSON 2

7 Complete the conversation. Use the correct preposition with the verb or adjective, and a gerund.

A: You look a little blue. What's up?

B: Oh, nothing really. I'm just ____*sick of working*____ late every night.
                                      1. sick / work

A: Is that all? You look really down.

B: I'm _____ the same thing every day. And I also feel
          2. bored / do

_____ too little time at home.
      3. sad / spend

A: Have you _____ overtime?
                   4. complained / work

B: No. I'm _____ my boss angry. I had to _____ a report
                 5. afraid / make   6. apologize / finish

late. And now my boss is _____ us more work.
                             7. talking / give

A: Wow! I see why you are feeling blue. Why don't you start looking for a new job?

B: Maybe I should.

FACTOID: Food to Improve Your Mood

Studies show that eating certain foods can help cheer you up when you are feeling blue. Eating foods that contain vitamins D and B and omega-3 fatty acids, such as fish, nuts, eggs, spinach, and bananas, increase the chemicals in your brain that make you feel happy and relaxed.

INFORMATION SOURCE: psychologytoday.com

8 **Suggest something to cheer the people up. Write complete sentences.**

I'm really tired of this job. I've been working late every night for a month!

1. _____
_____
_____

A rainy Monday always puts me in a bad mood.

2. _____
_____
_____

I'm really upset that I don't have enough money to go on a trip abroad this year.

3. _____
_____
_____

I've been feeling blue lately. I'm just bored with life.

4. _____
_____
_____

LESSON 3

9 **Extra reading comprehension**

Read the article on page 80 of the Student's Book again. Then answer the questions.

1. What are people with easygoing personalities like? _____
_____

2. What type of personality is the opposite of easygoing? _____
_____

3. Why is it difficult to settle the "nature-nurture controversy"? _____
_____

4. Where do most experts believe our personalities come from? _____
_____

5. Do you think nature or nurture is more important in forming personality? Explain your answer.
_____
_____

10 Read the posts on an online message board. Rank the people from 1 to 5, with 1 being the least introverted and 5 being the most extroverted.

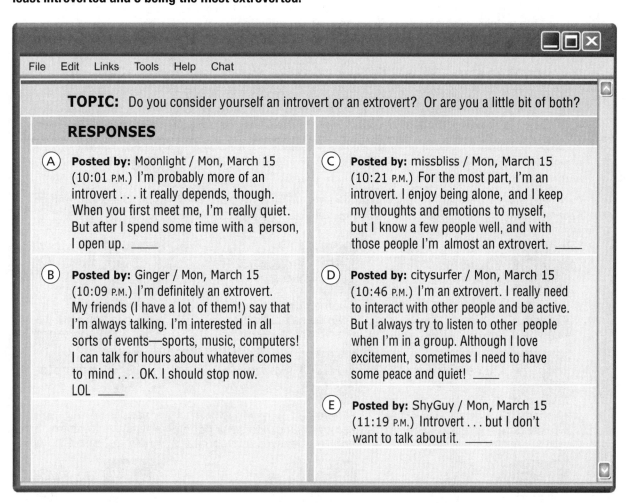

TOPIC: Do you consider yourself an introvert or an extrovert? Or are you a little bit of both?

RESPONSES

(A) **Posted by:** Moonlight / Mon, March 15 (10:01 P.M.) I'm probably more of an introvert . . . it really depends, though. When you first meet me, I'm really quiet. But after I spend some time with a person, I open up. _____

(B) **Posted by:** Ginger / Mon, March 15 (10:09 P.M.) I'm definitely an extrovert. My friends (I have a lot of them!) say that I'm always talking. I'm interested in all sorts of events—sports, music, computers! I can talk for hours about whatever comes to mind . . . OK. I should stop now. LOL _____

(C) **Posted by:** missbliss / Mon, March 15 (10:21 P.M.) For the most part, I'm an introvert. I enjoy being alone, and I keep my thoughts and emotions to myself, but I know a few people well, and with those people I'm almost an extrovert. _____

(D) **Posted by:** citysurfer / Mon, March 15 (10:46 P.M.) I'm an extrovert. I really need to interact with other people and be active. But I always try to listen to other people when I'm in a group. Although I love excitement, sometimes I need to have some peace and quiet! _____

(E) **Posted by:** ShyGuy / Mon, March 15 (11:19 P.M.) Introvert . . . but I don't want to talk about it. _____

11 Are you an introvert, an extrovert, or a little of both? Write your own reply to the message board topic in Exercise 10.

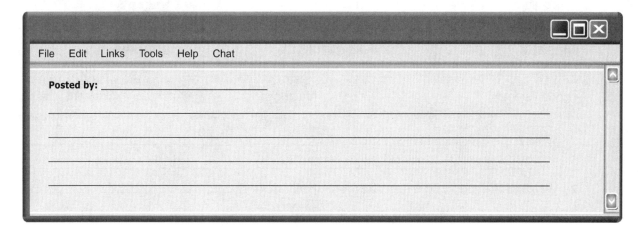

Posted by: _____

_____

_____

_____

_____

12 Read the article about astrology. Then answer the questions.

ASTROLOGY -FINDING YOUR PERSONALITY IN THE STARS

Why do you act the way you do? What is the secret to your emotions? Where does your personality come from? Is it nature or nurture? Genetics or the environment? Or could it be the sun and the stars?

Some people think that birth order influences personality, but many others believe that the day you were born on influences your personality. These people believe in astrology. They believe that the sun and the stars influence human personality and events.

Astrology may be a way to understand human personality. Or it may be a false science. But millions of people around the world read their astrological horoscope every day—just in case!

Aquarius ♒
Jan 20–Feb 18

• very active
• cheerful
• can be a clown

Gemini ♊
May 21–Jun 21

• worries about things
• can be self-critical
• can be hard to know

Libra ♎
Sept 23–Oct 23

• conservative
• spends time with a few friends
• has strong emotions

Pisces ♓
Feb 19–Mar 20

• honest
• easily bored with jobs
• likes quiet time

Cancer ♋
Jun 22–Jul 22

• interested in travel
• enjoys being with other people
• always behaves appropriately

Scorpio ♏
Oct 24–Nov 21

• friendly
• sensitive to others' emotions
• not easy to get to know

Aries ♈
Mar 21–Apr 19

• enjoys being alone
• hard to get to know
• keeps thoughts and emotions inside

Leo ♌
Jul 23–Aug 22

• happy with lots of people
• cheers people up
• crazy about nature

Sagittarius ♐
Nov 22–Dec 21

• creative
• likes everything in moderation
• gets along with everyone

Taurus ♉
Apr 20–May 20

• calm
• seeks peace
• good listener

Virgo ♍
Aug 23–Sept 22

• keeps ideas inside
• likes to spend time alone
• enjoys reading

Capricorn ♑
Dec 22–Jan 19

• has a lot of friends
• interested in events
• loves excitement

1. What is the basic idea behind astrology? _____

_____

2. Which of the zodiac signs describe more of an introvert? _____

3. Which signs describe more of an extrovert? _____

4. What zodiac sign are you? _____ Does the description for your sign describe

you? Why or why not? _____

_____

5. Compare the personality traits for your birth order with the personality traits for your zodiac sign. Are there any similarities? Which describes you better?

_____

_____

_____

GRAMMAR BOOSTER

A Complete each sentence with a gerund or an infinitive. Use verbs from the box. If either a gerund or an infinitive is correct, write both forms.

cook	do	drink	play	ride	study	watch

1. Susan can't stand _____ the dishes after dinner.

2. Michael loves _____ the guitar.

3. Marianna hates _____ for exams.

4. Joseph would like _____ his bike.

5. Beth doesn't mind _____ for her family.

6. Jim likes _____ TV.

7. My friend Jane avoids _____ whole milk.

B Unscramble the words and phrases to complete the conversations. Use a gerund or an infinitive.

1. **A:** John _can't stand thinking about graduation_____ .
   think / about / can't stand / graduation

   B: I know. _____ .
   He / leave / hates / his friends

2. **A:** _____ .
   refuse / dinner / tonight / I / make

   B: Fine by me. _____ .
   don't mind / go / I / out to eat

3. **A:** _____ ?
   buy / discussed / Have / you and Peter / a house

   B: Yes. _____ .
   find / We / would like / something bigger

4. **A:** _____ .
   tonight / you / I / see / didn't expect

   B: Well, _____ .
   at the last minute / I / decided / come

C Complete each sentence. Circle the letter.

1. I love _____ TV in the evening.
   a. watch   b. to watch   c. watched

2. I hurt my knee last month, so I quit _____.
   a. jog   b. to jog   c. jogging

3. _____ too many sweets is bad for you.
   a. Eating   b. Eat   c. Eaten

4. My favorite thing to do after work is _____ magazines.
   a. read   b. to reading   c. to read

5. If you get an early start, you'll have a better chance of _____ your work on time.
   a. finish   b. finishing   c. to finish

6. I don't mind _____ the window. It's freezing in here!
   a. closing   b. close   c. closed

7. _____ opera well is a hard thing to do.
   a. Sing   b. To sing   c. To singing

D Find and correct seven errors in the diary.

Usually I don't mind studying, but last night I was so sick of do homework that I decided to go out with Amy. She felt like go to the movies. I suggested a new romantic comedy that I'm excited about to see. But Amy said she can't stand romantic movies and suggested to watch an action movie instead. To me, watch violence is not appealing. So, finally, we agreed trying an animated film from Japan. We both found it really enjoyable. We're planning rent some other anime films to watch this weekend.

E Complete each sentence with an affirmative or negative gerund.

1. You should start _____ every day if you want to lose weight.
   exercise

2. Sue was worried about _____ enough money to pay her bills.
   have

3. When will you finish _____ on that project?
   work

4. Avoid _____ a cell phone while you're driving.
   use

5. Stella and I have considered _____ a new car. We just don't have the money.
   buy

6. I apologize for _____ you that I'd be late. I'm sorry that you've waited so long.
   tell

7. Let's start _____. I'm going to love _____ at that old wallpaper anymore!
   paint   *look*

8. Natalie has been working very long hours lately. She's depressed about _____ much time with her family.
   spend

9. I suggest _____ fatty foods. You'll be healthier.
   eat

WRITING BOOSTER

A Complete each sentence. Circle the letter. Be careful to use parallel structure. One item has two correct answers.

1. Robert has begun to exercise, eat a healthy diet, and _____ plenty of sleep.
   a. getting   b. to get   c. get

2. Julia hates working long hours and _____ enough time with her family.
   a. not spending   b. to not spend   c. not spend

3. Virgos like to read and _____ time alone.
   a. spending   b. to spend   c. spend

4. Although he has been seeing a psychologist, he continues to feel down, to avoid interaction with others, and _____ all the time.
   a. feeling tired   b. to feel tired   c. feel tired

5. Enjoying being alone, being hard to get to know, and _____ and emotions inside are traits typical of an Aries.
   a. keeping thoughts   b. to keep thoughts   c. keep thoughts

6. Some typical behaviors of a middle child are to break rules, have a lot of friends, and _____ rebellious.
   a. being   b. to be   c. be

B Answer the questions about your own likes, dislikes, and personality. Answer in complete sentences, using words and phrases from Unit 7. Be careful to use parallel structure.

1. What are your likes? _____

2. What are your dislikes? _____

3. Which extrovert personality traits do you have? _____

4. Which introvert personality traits do you have? _____

5. What is your birth position in your family? _____

6. Which traits for this position describe you? _____

7. What is your zodiac sign? _____

8. Which traits for this sign describe you? _____

C On a separate sheet of paper, write at least two paragraphs about your personality. In the first paragraph, tell something about yourself. In the second paragraph, discuss where you think your personality traits come from—nature, nurture, birth order, and / or astrology.

1 Look at the paintings and read the conversation. Then read the statements and check <u>true</u> or <u>false</u>.

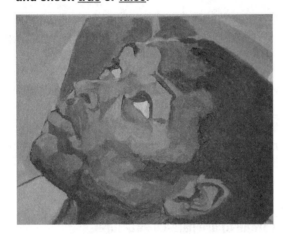

Serena by Jessica Miller-Smith

Thoughts by Agnes Geniusaite

Sophie: Is this painting by Jessica Miller-Smith? I had no idea she had so much talent!

Gerald: She doesn't really look like the artistic type, does she?

Sophie: I guess you can't always judge a book by its cover. It's really quite good. What do you think?

Gerald: I find it a little weird, actually. It makes me feel nervous.

Sophie: But that's what makes it interesting. In my opinion, it's exciting.

Gerald: Hey, this is an interesting piece. It's by Agnes Geniusaite. I love her work.

Sophie: I think it's kind of depressing.

Gerald: You do? Maybe you're just feeling a little blue today.

Sophie: No, I mean it. I guess I'm just not really into all the dark colors.

Gerald: Well, to each his own, I guess.

	true	false
1. Gerald is really into Jessica Miller-Smith's painting.	☐	☐
2. Sophie likes Miller-Smith.	☐	☐
3. Gerald is a fan of Agnes Geniusaite's art.	☐	☐
4. Sophie finds Geniusaite's painting depressing.	☐	☐
5. Sophie prefers darker colors to brighter colors.	☐	☐
6. Sophie and Gerald like the same kind of art.	☐	☐

2 Write a plus (+) next to the statements that indicate that the person likes the art, and a minus (-) next to the statements that indicate that the person doesn't like it.

1. _____ I had no idea he had so much talent.

2. _____ Her work is very impressive.

3. _____ This abstract sculpture is fascinating.

4. _____ It's an unforgettable photograph.

5. _____ I find it a little boring, actually.

6. _____ I guess I'm just not really into modern art.

7. _____ It's a little weird, but that's what makes it so interesting.

8. _____ This is an unusual piece, but I don't find it appealing.

3 What do Sophie and Gerald think of the paintings in Exercise 1? Complete the chart.

	Miller-Smith	Geniusaite
Sophie's opinion		
Gerald's opinion		

4 CHALLENGE. Which painting in Exercise 1 do you prefer? Why? Write a few sentences expressing your opinion.

LESSON 1

5 Read each sentence and decide if it is in the active voice (<u>A</u>) or passive voice (<u>P</u>).

1. _____ Many people visit the Metropolitan Museum of Art in New York.

2. _____ The glass pyramid in front of the Louvre was finished in 1989.

3. _____ A color poster of the painting was made available.

4. _____ The museum catalog has been translated into many languages.

5. _____ Akira Kurosawa directed the film *Seven Samurai* in 1954.

6. _____ That vase was made in ancient Egypt.

7. _____ The photograph was taken fifty years ago.

8. _____ Matisse painted *La Musique* in 1910.

6 Use the information in the chart to write two sentences, one in the active voice and one in the passive voice. Be sure to use the correct verb with the artwork.

Art Object	Artist	Year
1. *Still Life with Watermelon* (painting)	Pablo Picasso	1946
2. *Vines and Olive Trees* (painting)	Joan Miró	1919
3. *The Raven and the First Men* (wood figure)	Bill Reid	1994
4. *Citizen Kane* (film)	Orson Welles	1941
5. *Waterfront Demonstration* (photograph)	Dorothea Lange	1934

1. **Active:** *Pablo Picasso painted Still Life with Watermelon in 1946.*

   Passive: *Still Life with Watermelon was painted by Pablo Picasso in 1946.*

2. **Active:** _____

   Passive: _____

3. **Active:** _____

   Passive: _____

4. **Active:** _____

   Passive: _____

5. **Active:** _____

   Passive: _____

7 Read a page from a tour guide about Paris. Complete the conversation. Make a recommendation to someone who is visiting Paris, using the information in the tour guide.

The Rodin Museum

There are many wonderful museums to see while you are visiting Paris. One museum you should be sure to visit is the lovely Rodin Museum. The Rodin Museum houses over 6,600 sculptures. There is also an impressive garden. A large number of sculptures are presented in this setting, including Rodin's most famous work, *The Thinker*. In addition to the sculptures, take a look at the excellent drawing collection. Many of Rodin's sketches are there.

YOU Be sure _____
1.
in Paris.

B: Really? Why's that?

YOU Well, _____.
2.

B: No kidding!

YOU They also _____
3.

_____.

You'll _____.
4.

B: Thanks for the recommendation.

INFORMATION SOURCE: musee-rodin.fr

8 Choose the correct response. Write the letter on the line.

1. _____ "Is this vase handmade?"

2. _____ "What do you think of this painting?"

3. _____ "Where was the figure made?"

4. _____ "Do you know when this photograph was taken?"

5. _____ "What's the bowl made of?"

a. Clay. It's handmade.

b. Yes, it is.

c. It says it was made in Bulgaria.

d. Not much. I'm not crazy about the colors.

e. Around 1980, I think.

9 Unscramble the words to write questions.

1. were / Where / built / those / wood chairs _____ ?

2. made of / are / those / bowls / What _____ ?

3. Were / painted / those / wood figures / by hand _____ ?

4. was / painted / When / that / mural _____ ?

5. this / made in Thailand / gold jewelry / Was _____ ?

6. are / What / these / used for / cloth bags _____ ?

10 Look at the pictures. Write sentences to describe the objects. Use words from the box or your own ideas.

Material	clay	cloth	glass	gold	stone	wood
Adjective	beautiful impressive	boring interesting	cool practical	depressing terrific	fantastic weird	fascinating wonderful

1. _The hat is made of cloth. It's fantastic._

2. _____

3. _____

4. _____

5. _____

6. _____

sombrero hat, Mexico

bag, Spain

elephant figure, India

rocking chair, Canada

balalaika guitar, Russia

vase, France

11 Read the article about how to develop artistic talent.

Nurturing Your Artistic Talent

1 So, you'd like to improve your artistic ability, but you think you don't have any natural talent? The truth is you don't have to be born with talent to be a good artist—and to enjoy making art. Artistic skill can be learned.

2 Many people who try painting get frustrated and give up because they feel they lack the "artistic gene." However, the real problem is that they have just never been trained to look at the world like an artist. When non-artists look at the subject of a drawing, they see it with the left side of their brains. They immediately begin figuring out the meaning of what they see. An artist pays attention to what is actually being seen—the lines. Are they straight or curved? Dark or light? Where do they intersect?

3 Want to learn to see like an artist? Try this exercise. Find a large photo of a face and try to draw it. It's OK if your drawing looks bad. Then turn the photo upside down and try again. This time focus only on the relationships of the intersecting lines and shapes. Almost always, the upside-down drawing, when turned right side up, will be much better than the right-side-up version! How did this happen? By turning the photo upside down, the left side of your brain stopped looking at the photo as a face. Instead, the right side of your brain took over and began seeing the photo in a new way.

4 People who claim they have no artistic talent may actually have talent. But they may not be able to use it because they worry, "What will people think? Will I look silly? Will my piece be awful?" Young children rarely have these fears. They just enjoy the experience of creating something. To be successful at art, you will need to adopt the carefree attitude that you once had as a child. Don't worry about the results. Just relax and enjoy the experience of creating art.

5 Anyone can develop the necessary skills and understanding to create art. Those with natural talent are able to learn more quickly and easily, but even they will need training, practice, and hard work. So, stop making excuses and get started! Take art lessons, read books on art, and attend art exhibits. Expose yourself to a variety of techniques, kinds of art, and other artists. And think of becoming an artist as a lifetime journey. Stop worrying about making mistakes and enjoy the adventure!

INFORMATION SOURCE: MasterPaintingLessons.com

12 **Answer the questions, according to the article in Exercise 11. Circle the letter.**

1. What is the main idea of paragraph 2?
   a. Lacking the "artistic gene" is a real problem.
   b. You should always draw faces upside down.
   c. It's important to learn to see like an artist.
   d. Try to use the left side of your brain when you draw.

2. What is the main idea of paragraph 4?
   a. Children are better artists than adults.
   b. Fear of making mistakes prevents many adults from creating art.
   c. Fear helps adults find their artistic talent.
   d. Beginners' artwork is usually silly.

3. What is the main idea of paragraph 5?
   a. Artists with natural talent don't have to work hard.
   b. It takes a very long time to become a good artist.
   c. Artistic ability can be improved by attending art shows.
   d. Anyone can make art with practice and hard work.

13 **Read the quotations by famous artists. Find a paragraph in the article that presents an opinion similar to that expressed by each artist. Write the number of the paragraph on the line.**

1. _____

"Every child is an artist. The problem is how to remain an artist once we grow up."
—Pablo Picasso

2. _____

"I am doubtful of any talent, so whatever I choose to be, will be accomplished only by long study and work."
—Jackson Pollock

3. _____

"Creation begins with vision. The artist has to look at everything as though seeing it for the first time."
—Henri Matisse

14 **Read the third paragraph of the article again. Try the drawing exercise on a separate sheet of paper. Then answer the questions.**

1. Which drawing was easier? _____

2. Which drawing took more time? _____

3. Which drawing looks more like the photograph? _____

4. Did the exercise help you to see more like an artist? Explain. _____

_____

15 **Complete the biography of Pablo Picasso using the passive voice.**

Pablo Ruiz Picasso began studying art with his father. Then from 1895 until 1904, he painted in Barcelona. During this time, he made his first trip to Paris, where he _____ by the
<u>1. inspire</u>
artwork of Henri de Toulouse-Lautrec. In Paris, Picasso _____ by all the poverty
<u>2. influence</u>
he saw. He was sad and angry that so many people lived without enough food or clothing. He painted many pictures of poor people to bring attention to their situation.

In 1906, Picasso met the artist Henri Matisse, who was to become his longtime friend. Picasso
_____ in Matisse's style, but he did not imitate it. The artists he really admired were
<u>3. interest</u>
Georges Braque and Joan Miró. Picasso _____ by Braque's and Miró's work.
<u>4. fascinate</u>
Together the three artists started the movement known as Cubism.

One of Picasso's most famous artistic pieces is
Guernica. Picasso _____ by the violence
<u>5. move</u>
of the Spanish Civil War. This prompted him to paint the piece.

16 **Read the biography in Exercise 16 again. Rewrite the five sentences in the passive voice, changing them to the active voice.**

1. _____
2. _____
3. _____
4. _____
5. _____

17 **CHALLENGE. Write a short paragraph about your favorite kind of art and your favorite artist. Use some of the phrases from the box.**

interested in	fascinated by	inspired by	moved by	influenced by

A If possible, rewrite the sentences, changing the active voice to the passive voice. If a sentence cannot be changed to the passive voice, circle the verb and write <u>intransitive</u> on the line.

1. Leonardo da Vinci painted the *Mona Lisa* in the 16th century.

   _____

2. Pablo Picasso died in 1973 at 91 years old.

   _____

3. Paul Klee used simple lines and strong colors in his many paintings.

   _____

4. The artist's later work seems quite dark and depressing.

   _____

5. A new exhibit of impressionist paintings arrives at the Philadelphia Museum of Art this summer.

   _____

6. Marc Jacobs will show his spring collection at New York Fashion Week.

   _____

7. In Florence, we walked from The Uffizi Gallery to the Accademia Gallery to see Michelangelo's *David*.

   _____

B Choose the best answer to complete each sentence. Circle the letter.

1. This vase _____ made in 1569.
   a. is   **b.** has been   **c.** was   **d.** was being

2. Today, coffee _____ grown in more than fifty countries worldwide.
   a. has been   **b.** will be   **c.** was   **d.** is

3. Right now, business cards _____ exchanged at the meeting.
   a. were   **b.** were being   **c.** are being   **d.** have been

4. The art exhibition _____ attended by over 1,000 people so far.
   a. was   **b.** has been   **c.** is going to be   **d.** is being

5. We probably _____ invited to the wedding. It's going to be very small.
   a. won't be   **b.** weren't being   **c.** haven't been   **d.** weren't

C Use the words to write sentences in the passive voice.

1. French / speak / in Quebec, Canada _____

2. The Taj Mahal / build / around 1631 _____

3. A new art museum / open / next year _____

4. Many products / make / in China _____

5. "Imagine" / write / by John Lennon _____

6. Your DVD player / repair / now _____

7. The *Mona Lisa* / see / by millions of people since it was painted _____

   _____

D Read the description of a museum. Find and correct four more mistakes in the use of the passive voice.

The Frick Collection

The mansion of Henry Clay Frick ~~builded~~ *was built* in 1914 at the corner of Fifth Avenue and

East 70th Street in New York City. It was later open to the public. Several improvements

have made over the years. Works of Manet, El Greco, Bernini, Degas, Vermeer, and many

other artists found throughout the mansion. Some of the museum's large collection of art

displayed at temporary exhibitions around the world.

E Rewrite the sentences in the passive voice. Use a <u>by</u> phrase only if it is important or necessary to know who or what is performing the action.

1. People in Guatemala carved this wood figure.

   _____

2. Artists hand-paint these plates in France.

   _____

3. Valentino is showing a lot of bright colors this season.

   _____

4. Stores everywhere are going to sell her jewelry.

   _____

5. Swiss companies still make the world's best watches.

   _____

6. Shakespeare wrote *King Lear*.

   _____

F Rewrite the sentences in the passive voice in Exercise E as <u>yes</u> / <u>no</u> questions.

1. *Was this wood figure carved in Guatemala?* _____
2. _____
3. _____
4. _____
5. _____
6. _____

A Read the paragraph. Underline the topic sentence. Circle the supporting details. Cross out the two sentences that don't belong.

I have been to museums in countries all over the world, but my favorite painting is in a museum close to my home. I am a real fan of *The Master's Bedroom* by Andrew Wyeth because I find it very peaceful. Andrew Wyeth died in 2009 at the age of 91. The painting shows a dog curled up on a bed, taking an afternoon nap. Sunlight is coming in through the window and warming the dog. The painting makes me feel relaxed because the dog and the bed look so comfortable. The bedroom is very simple and the colors in the painting are soft and neutral, making the scene seem really calm. Wyeth's most famous painting is *Christina's World,* which is at the Museum of Modern Art in New York City.

B Think about your favorite painting. Answer the questions.

1. What is the title of the painting? _____

2. Who is the artist? _____

3. Why do you like it? _____

_____

C Prepare to describe your favorite painting in a paragraph. Create a topic sentence and supporting details.

a. What is the most important thing you want to say about the painting?

_____

b. Write five sentences to support your topic sentence.

1. _____

2. _____

3. _____

4. _____

5. _____

D On a separate sheet of paper, write a paragraph describing your favorite painting. Feel free to change the order of your sentences, or add more details, if you think it improves your writing.

Living with Computers

1 Read the Photo Story on page 99 of the Student's Book again. Then answer the questions.

1. What computer problem does Amy have? _____

_____

2. What solution does Dee suggest? _____

_____

2 Read the instant message conversation.
Then answer the questions.

ron22: Hey, Deb. Are you there?

dpike: Hi, Ron. Just catching up on e-mail.

ron22: Am I interrupting you?

dpike: Not at all. What's up?

ron22: I logged on to send you some pictures.

dpike: Great! What of?

ron22: Photos of my trip!!!

dpike: Cool! Can't wait to see them.

ron22: It'll just be a second . . .

B I U A A A A A ♫ ♥ SEND

a few minutes later

dpike: Hi Ron, still there? I didn't get the pix.

ron22: Sorry! I attached the photos, but I can't send the message. It says the files are too large!

dpike: Maybe you should try sending them one at a time.

ron22: You think that would work?

dpike: It usually does the trick.

ron22: OK, I'll try it.

B I U A A A A A ♫ ♥ SEND

1. What computer problem does Ron have? _____

_____

2. What solution does Deb suggest? _____

_____

3 Which of the following computer problems have you experienced?

☐ computer won't start   ☐ lost a file   ☐ printer won't print

☐ computer is slowing down   ☐ got a computer virus   ☐ can't log on

☐ keyboard freezes   ☐ mouse doesn't work   ☐ can't attach a file

4 CHALLENGE. Have you ever asked someone for help with a computer problem? If so, who did you ask? What solution did the person suggest?

5 Choose the correct response. Circle the letter.

1. "What are you doing here at this hour?"
   a. Nothing happens.   b. Running antivirus software.   c. I've never had a problem before.

2. "Am I interrupting you?"
   a. Of course.   b. Right.   c. Not at all.

3. "When I try to click on an icon, my computer freezes and won't do anything."
   a. It couldn't hurt.   b. Sometimes that does the trick.   c. Maybe you should try rebooting.

4. "You think that would fix the problem?"
   a. It couldn't hurt.   b. I'll just be a second.   c. Sorry to hear that.

LESSON 1

6 Use the icon prompts to complete the conversation. Write the word on the line.

A: Could you take a look at this?

B: Sure. What's the problem?

A: Well, I clicked on the toolbar to _____ 1. my document, and now everything is gone!

B: Don't worry. You probably accidentally clicked on the _____ 2. icon. Just move your cursor over there and click on this icon to _____ 3. it.

A: Oh . . . There it is! Thank you!

7 Complete each sentence with a word from the box.

click on	cut	paste	print	save	scroll down	select	toolbar

1. Oh, no! I just lost all the work I've done on this document because I forgot to _____ the file.

2. You can't _____ if the printer is not turned on.

3. To _____ a word, move the cursor over the word and highlight it.

4. You don't have to type the entire paragraph again. Just copy and _____ it where you need it.

5. I tried to _____ the icon but nothing happened. What did I do wrong?

6. The _____ has a list of icons that provide a quick way to use computer commands.

7. To see more information on the product, _____ to the bottom of the page.

8. Your article is great but a little too long. Could you _____ a few paragraphs?

8 Match each action with the correct purpose. Write the letter on the line.

1. _____ He enrolled in an electronics course because he . . .   a. needed to buy a printer.

2. _____ She went to the electronics store because she . . .   b. needed to be more organized.

3. _____ I bought speakers because I . . .   c. wanted to learn how to repair computers.

4. _____ He turned on the television because he . . .   d. wanted to listen to music on the computer.

5. _____ She bought a smart phone because she . . .   e. wanted to watch the news.

9 Rewrite the sentences in Exercise 8, using infinitives of purpose.

1. _____

2. _____

3. _____

4. _____

5. _____

LESSON 2

10 Put the conversation in order. Write the number on the line.

__1__ I was wondering if you could help me with something.

_____ Why don't you get an OptiMouse? I have one and I really like it.

_____ Well, I'm thinking about buying a new mouse, but I'm not sure which one to get.

_____ Then how about the UltraClick? It's nearly as easy to use as the OptiMouse, but it doesn't cost quite as much.

_____ Of course. What's up?

_____ I like the OptiMouse, but it's a little expensive.

__7__ Sounds good. I'll have to check it out.

11 Look at the chart comparing two laptop computers. Complete the sentences, using (not) as . . . as and the adjectives. Use the adverbs almost, quite, just, and nearly.

	Ace EC650u laptop	Simsun B400 laptop
Price	$619	$599
Weight	5 pounds / 2.3 kilograms	3 pounds / 1.4 kilograms
Screen size	16 inches / 40.6 centimeters	15.5 inches / 39.4 centimeters
Screen quality		
Touchpad ease of use		
Speed		
Speaker quality		
Noise		

KEY

Better

↕

Worse

1. The quality of the Ace screen is ___just as good as___ the quality of the Simsun screen.
   good
2. The Simsun laptop is _____ the Ace laptop.
   expensive
3. The Simsun touchpad isn't _____ the Ace touchpad.
   easy to use
4. The Simsun laptop is _____ the Ace laptop.
   fast
5. The Ace speakers are _____ the Simsun speakers.
   good
6. The Ace laptop isn't _____ the Simsun laptop.
   light
7. The Simsun screen isn't _____ the Ace screen.
   large

12 CHALLENGE. Which laptop in Exercise 11 would you buy? Explain your reasons, using (not) as . . . as and some of the adverbs from Exercise 11.

13 Read about how the people use computers. Complete the statements with words from the box.

send instant messages	surf the Internet	join an online group
upload photos	download music files	

1.

"I'm a designer, and I really need to learn about what people wear and why they wear it. So I decided to _____ called Fashion Friends. On the website I discuss clothing trends and style with other members."

2.

"I have a lot of friends and I like to be in touch with them all the time. Talking on the phone isn't always practical, and e-mail is too slow. So, my friends and I _____ to each other all the time."

3.

"I'm a huge music fan, but I never buy CDs at a music store. I _____ from the Internet, instead. I've got almost 10,000 songs on my MP3 player now!"

4.

"I'm spending two months traveling through Europe. I want my friends and family to see all the fascinating places I'm visiting, so I _____ from my laptop to a website where everyone can view them."

5.

"I spend about eight hours a day online. I usually just _____, clicking from one website to another without any real plan. I love to discover new and different websites about things that interest me."

14 CHALLENGE. On a separate sheet of paper, write a paragraph about how you use computers. Be sure to answer the following questions.

- How many hours a week do you spend on a computer?
- Do you spend more or less time on a computer than your friends or family members?
- Do you use a computer more for work or for fun?
- What do you use a computer to do?

15 Read the article from a career advice website.

File   Edit   Links   Tools   Help   Chat

Social Networking: Could It Hurt Your Job Search?

PRIVACY

To be the best candidate for a job, you'll need more than an impressive résumé and a nice suit. You also need to make sure there isn't any information about you online that could cause an employer not to hire you. A recent study found that 77 percent of recruiters search the Internet for information about applicants they are considering for a job. Thirty-five percent of these same recruiters say they have rejected an applicant based on information they have found online.

"A profile on a social networking site can show you a lot more of a person's character than a résumé," says Jen Romney, a corporate recruiter who recently began looking up the names of applicants on the Web. "It's surprising what you can find. I once had to make a difficult decision between two excellent applicants. When I found one of the applicants' profile on a social networking site, the decision became much easier. The man's profile was full of negative comments about his job and boss. In one post he wrote, 'I'm calling in sick today—because I'm sick of work!' I don't need to tell you that he didn't get the job."

Romney warns that as people share more of their lives online, it becomes harder to keep one's private life completely private. "Everything is public," says Romney. "It's called the World Wide Web for a reason. Anyone in the world can see it."

While not all employers research potential employees online, it's worth being a little careful to make sure that social networking doesn't ruin your career opportunities. You can protect yourself by following four simple rules:

1. **Think before you click.** Before you post photos of you and your friends partying or comments about how you hate your job, ask yourself: Would I be comfortable talking about this in a job interview?

2. **Take control.** Most social networking sites have privacy controls. Take the time to figure them out and use them wisely. Set your controls so that only people you've chosen as "friends" can view your profile and post messages on your page.

3. **Review.** Check your profile regularly to see what has been posted. Type your name and e-mail address into a search engine to see what is on the Internet about you.

4. **Delete.** Remove any potentially embarrassing or offensive posts, information, or photos. Ask friends to delete anything inappropriate about you on their own profiles.

INFORMATION SOURCE: CareerBuilder.com

16 Use the context of the article to match the terms with their meanings.

1. _____ recruiter
2. _____ search engine
3. _____ profile
4. _____ post
5. _____ private

a. only for a particular group to see, not for everyone

b. information, photos, comments, etc. put on a website

c. a person who finds candidates to fill jobs

d. page on a social networking site with a member's personal information

e. a program that helps you find things on the Internet

17 Answer the questions, according to the information in the article in Exercise 15.

1. How does the Internet make it easier for employers to get information about job applicants?

    _____

    _____

2. What type of information in an online profile can hurt a job applicant's chances of getting a job?

    _____

    _____

3. What is one way you can control who is able to view your online profiles?

    _____

    _____

4. How can you learn what information is available about you online?

    _____

    _____

18 CHALLENGE. Do you think the article in Exercise 15 gives good advice? What have you done, or what do you plan to do, to protect your image online? Explain your answer.

GRAMMAR BOOSTER

A Read the conversation. Find all the infinitives that express a purpose. Underline the sentences.

A: It's 6:00. Are you going home?

B: No, I'm staying late to finish this report. How about you?

A: I'm leaving now. I'm going to stop at Big Box to buy a new printer. Then I'm going to ComputerWorld to get something else on sale.

B: Really? What?

A: I'm thinking about getting a new laptop.

B: What's wrong with your home computer?

A: Nothing. But the kids use it to surf the Internet all the time.

B: What do they do online?

A: Oh, everything. They use the computer to check e-mail, download music, chat with their friends, and play games.

B Rewrite the sentences you underlined in Exercise A. Use <u>in order to</u>.

1. _____
2. _____
3. _____
4. _____
5. _____

C Rewrite Speaker A's last sentence in Exercise A again, using <u>for</u>. (Remember to change the verbs into gerunds.)

_____

_____

D Complete the sentences with <u>for</u> or <u>to</u>.

1. I like to shop online _____ delicious foods from Italy.

2. My son uses the computer _____ download music.

3. Judith e-mailed me _____ directions to the party.

4. Daniel uses the Internet _____ get the latest news.

5. Sheila e-mailed her mother _____ say she bought a new computer.

E Complete the sentences. Use an infinitive of purpose or <u>for</u>.

1. I use the Internet _____.

2. I'd buy a new printer _____.

3. I'd get a new smart phone _____.

F Complete each sentence with the correct form of the adjective or adverb.

1. I shop online for computer products. It's much _____ than going to a computer store.

easy

2. My brother plays music _____ than anyone I know.

loudly

3. Of all the printers in the store, the R100 is definitely the _____.

quiet

4. This is the _____ movie I've ever seen.

romantic

5. Jessica's oil paintings are beautiful. Her pencil drawings are just as _____.

impressive

6. Believe it or not, this new laptop works as _____ as the old one.

badly

7. The Bax monitor is not large enough. I need something even _____.

big

8. The traffic on my way to work was very slow. Luckily, the traffic on my way home was not nearly as

   _____.

bad

9. We've never had a _____ vacation than this one. It was so much fun!

exciting

10. Of the three printers we looked at, the XP prints the _____.

poorly

G Look at the video game reviews. Write sentences comparing the A–1 and Game Plan games. Use the comparative form of the adjective or adverb.

Video Game Reports **A–1**

	0 ←————→ 10
Sound quality	(5)
Visual quality	(8)
Interest level	(4)
Fun level	(6)
Violence level	(8)
Easy to play	(4)
Speed	(7)
Price	$89.95

Video Game Reports **Game Plan**

	0 ←————→ 10
Sound quality	(4)
Visual quality	(5)
Interest level	(8)
Fun level	(6)
Violence level	(7)
Easy to play	(7)
Speed	(4)
Price	$129.95

1. A–1 sounds _better than_ Game Plan.
   good
2. A–1 looks _____ Game Plan.
   good
3. Game Plan is _____ A–1.
   interesting
4. Game Plan is _____ A–1.
   violent
5. Game Plan is _____ A–1.
   easy to play
6. Game Plan runs _____ A–1.
   slow
7. A–1 is _____ Game Plan.
   expensive

H Now look at the review of a third video game. Write sentences comparing all three video games, using the superlative form of the adjective or adverb.

Video Game Reports **Top Game**

	0 ←————→ 10
Sound quality	(8)
Visual quality	(8)
Interest level	(2)
Fun level	(2)
Violence level	(5)
Easy to play	(3)
Speed	(8)
Price	$199.95

1. _Top Game sounds the best._
   good
2. _____
   expensive
3. _____
   fast
4. _____
   easy to play
5. _____
   interesting
6. _____
   violent

A Read the ideas for a piece of writing about the pros and cons of social networking. Then write the ideas in the appropriate place on the chart.

Ideas

- It's a great way to keep in touch with friends and family all over the world.
- You can find old friends and people you've lost contact with.
- It may be too entertaining—it's easy to waste a lot of time on social networking sites.
- Your friends may post photos or comments you'd rather not have others see.
- People you don't want to keep in touch with (like an old boyfriend or girlfriend) may ask to be your friend.
- Social networking is entertaining—and, on some sites, you can also play games and take fun quizzes.

Topic	Ideas	
1. communicating with family and friends	Pros	
	Cons	
2. getting back in touch with old friends	Pros	
	Cons	
3. is entertaining	Pros	
	Cons	

B On a separate sheet of paper, write two paragraphs about "The Pros and Cons of Social Networking." Use approach 2 from page 147 in the Student's Book. Use the ideas from the "Pros" row of the chart in paragraph 1. Use the ideas from the "Cons" row of the chart in paragraph 2. Create your own topic sentence for each paragraph.

C On a separate sheet of paper, use Approach 3. Use the ideas from row 1 of the chart in paragraph 1, the ideas from row 2 in paragraph 2, and the ideas from row 3 in paragraph 3. Create your own topic sentence for each paragraph. Use In addition and Furthermore to add your own ideas.

1 Read the messages to an advice columnist. What advice do you think the columnist will give? Check the box.

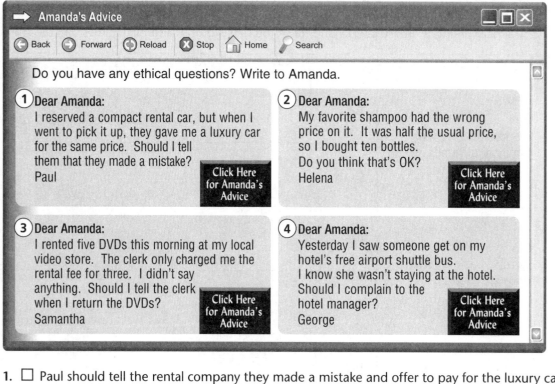

> → Amanda's Advice
>
> Back | Forward | Reload | Stop | Home | Search
>
> Do you have any ethical questions? Write to Amanda.
>
> **1** Dear Amanda:
> I reserved a compact rental car, but when I went to pick it up, they gave me a luxury car for the same price. Should I tell them that they made a mistake?
> Paul
>
> Click Here for Amanda's Advice
>
> **2** Dear Amanda:
> My favorite shampoo had the wrong price on it. It was half the usual price, so I bought ten bottles.
> Do you think that's OK?
> Helena
>
> Click Here for Amanda's Advice
>
> **3** Dear Amanda:
> I rented five DVDs this morning at my local video store. The clerk only charged me the rental fee for three. I didn't say anything. Should I tell the clerk when I return the DVDs?
> Samantha
>
> Click Here for Amanda's Advice
>
> **4** Dear Amanda:
> Yesterday I saw someone get on my hotel's free airport shuttle bus.
> I know she wasn't staying at the hotel. Should I complain to the hotel manager?
> George
>
> Click Here for Amanda's Advice

1. ☐ Paul should tell the rental company they made a mistake and offer to pay for the luxury car.
   ☐ Paul should stop worrying and enjoy his luxury car.
2. ☐ Helena should feel great about saving money.
   ☐ Helena should go back and tell the store manager the price was wrong and pay the correct price.
3. ☐ Samantha should tell the clerk that she wasn't charged for two DVDs.
   ☐ Samantha should just relax and enjoy the DVDs without telling the clerk.
4. ☐ George should tell the hotel manager about the person using the shuttle bus.
   ☐ George should mind his own business and not complain about someone else.

2 **CHALLENGE. Have you ever experienced a moral dilemma similar to the ones described in Exercise 1? Write a letter to Amanda about your situation.**

3 Read the conversations. Summarize the advice with real conditional sentences.

1. **A:** I don't have antivirus software.
   B: You shouldn't surf the Internet.

   If you don't have antivirus software, you shouldn't surf the Internet.

2. **A:** I want to e-mail old photos to friends.
   B: You have to scan them first.

   _____

3. **A:** I want to make friends on the Internet.
   B: You can join an online group.

   _____

4. **A:** My computer crashes all the time.
   B: You'd better find out what's wrong.

   _____

4 Rewrite the real conditional sentences in the unreal conditional. Use the true statements in parentheses to help you.

1. If we go to Russia, I'll learn Russian. (We're not going to Russia.)

   _____

2. If she has time, she'll study more. (She doesn't have time.)

   _____

3. If I need to lose weight, I'll avoid fatty foods. (I don't need to lose weight.)

   _____

4. If he's late, he won't get a seat. (He's never late.)

   _____

5 Match the two parts of each conditional sentence. Write the letter on the line.

1. _____ If you speak Spanish, you . . .
2. _____ If you spoke Spanish, you . . .
3. _____ Your hair will look great if you . . .
4. _____ He would look great if he . . .
5. _____ If you took a taxi, you . . .
6. _____ If you miss the bus, you . . .
7. _____ You'll get sunburned if you . . .
8. _____ We would get sunburned if we . . .

a. don't use sunscreen.
b. could work in South America.
c. won't get to work on time.
d. stayed at the beach too long.
e. use this shampoo every day.
f. can travel all over Central America.
g. got a haircut.
h. would get to work faster.

6 Complete each present unreal conditional sentence. Use your own ideas.

1. If I lived to be 100, _____.

2. My family would be angry if _____.

3. If I went to my favorite store, _____.

7 Look at the pictures. Use the words and phrases in the box to complete the conversations.

too much change	undercharged	didn't charge

1. **A:** Look at this bill.

   B: What's wrong with it?

   A: They _____ us. Look.
   They _____ us for the drinks
   or for the desserts.

   B: I guess we'd better tell them.

2. **A:** What's wrong?

   B: I think the clerk gave me _____.
   I should have only two euros back in change,
   but she gave me twelve!

   A: I'll try to get her attention . . . Excuse me?

LESSON 2

8 Circle the correct words to complete the conversations.

1. **A:** Where should we watch the game after work?

   B: Let's go to your house. (Your / Yours) TV is much bigger than (my / mine).

2. **A:** Is this (our / ours) room?

   B: No, we have a suite, and this is a single. So, this is definitely not (our / ours).

3. **A:** Is this car key (your / yours)?

   B: No, it's not (my / mine). I don't even have a car!

4. **A:** (Who / Whose) books are these? (Him / His) or (her / hers)?

   B: I don't know. Ask them if they're (their / theirs).

5. **A:** (Who / Whose) has traveled more? Your parents or (mine / my)?

   B: (Your / Yours) parents, I think. (My / Mine) parents don't travel much at all.

9 **Rewrite each sentence, using a possessive pronoun.**

1. The shaving cream is George's. _The shaving cream is his._____

2. The hair spray is Judy's. _____

3. The toothbrushes are Amy and Mark's. _____

4. The razors are George's. _____

5. The shampoo is everyone's. _____

10 **Look at the pictures. Complete the conversations with possessive adjectives or possessive pronouns.**

1. **A:** Excuse me. I think you forgot something.

   B: I did?

   A: Isn't that cell phone _____?

   B: No, it isn't. It must be _____.

2. **A:** Is this _____?

   B: No, it's not _____.

   It's _____ tip.

3. **A:** Is that book _____?

   B: No, it's _____ book.

4. **A:** Are these earrings _____?

   B: No, they're not _____.

   They're _____.

11 Read about the people's personal values. How would you describe each person?
Use words from the box or your own words. Explain your opinions.

modesty	sexist	old-fashioned	double-standard

James

> I hate having a female boss. I just don't think women make good managers.

_____

_____

_____

Dina

> I'm not comfortable wearing clothes that show too much of my body.

_____

_____

_____

Tessa

> I think it's fine for young men and women to get their bodies pierced if they want to. But if you're over forty, you really shouldn't. It just looks silly!

_____

_____

_____

Hazel

> People used to dress formally when they went to the opera. Now some people wear jeans. It's just not appropriate!

_____

_____

_____

12 CHALLENGE. Choose one person from Exercise 11. Do you have the same values?
Explain why or why not.

LESSON 4

13 Read the news stories on page 118 of the Student's Book again. Then answer the questions.

1. How did Kim Bogue lose her wallet? _____

_____

2. How did the homeless man return the wallet to her? _____

_____

3. What happened to Cameron Hollopeter? _____

_____

4. What did Wesley Autrey do? _____

_____

5. How did the airport screener figure out who the money belonged to? _____

_____

14 Read the news story about an act of honesty.

Pro Golfer J. P. Hayes's Act of Honesty

J. P. Hayes is a professional golfer. But Hayes has perhaps gotten more attention for an act of honesty than for his golf game. While playing in the first round of a PGA tournament in Texas, Hayes' caddie handed him a ball from his golf bag. Hayes took two shots and then noticed the ball he was playing with was a different model than the ball he started the round with. This is against the rules in professional golf. So, Hayes asked an official to come over and told him about his mistake. The official said the penalty for the mistake was two shots. Even with the penalty, Hayes finished with a good score. He also did well in the second round and had a good chance of advancing to the final. Hayes had struggled with his game that year, so this tournament was important to his career.

After the second round of the tournament, Hayes was relaxing in his hotel room when he realized there might be another problem with the ball he played in the first round. He realized it was a new type of ball that probably wasn't approved for competition by the United States Golf Association. Hayes's had tested the new balls for a golf equipment company four weeks earlier. Apparently, one was left in his bag by accident.

Hayes knew that if he admitted his mistake, he would probably not be allowed to play full-time on the next year's PGA tour. He also knew that no one except himself was aware of his mistake. Hayes had a choice: He could say nothing and keep playing, or he could admit that he had broken the rules and hurt his career.

Hayes decided to do the right thing. He called an official that night and, as expected, was disqualified from playing on the next PGA tour. Speaking about his mistake, Hayes said "It's extremely disappointing. I keep thinking I'm going to wake up and this is going to be a bad nightmare." However, Hayes never regretted his decision. "I would say everybody out here would have done the same thing," he asserted. But the real question is: Would they? In a similar situation, would other professional athletes have acted as honestly as J. P. Hayes?

INFORMATION SOURCE: JSOnline.com

Ethics and Values   **89**

15 Answer the questions, according to the article in Exercise 14.

1. What was the first mistake Hayes made? _____
   _____
   _____

3. Did anyone see Hayes make the mistakes? _____
   _____

4. What happened when Hayes told officials about the first mistake? _____
   _____

5. What happened when Hayes told officials about the second mistake? _____
   _____

16 CHALLENGE. Imagine that you had been in J. P. Hayes's situation. What would you have done? Answer the questions.

1. What could you do?	
2. What should you do?	
3. What would <u>you</u> do?	
4. What would most people do?	

GRAMMAR BOOSTER

A Read the statements and then complete the factual conditional sentences.

1. I usually go jogging every day, unless it rains.
   If it doesn't rain, _I go jogging_____.

2. I like driving short distances, but for longer distances, I always fly.
   _____ if I have to travel longer distances.

3. I never drink coffee after dinner. I can't fall asleep when I do.
   _____, I can't fall asleep at night.

4. It rarely snows here. The schools close whenever more than a centimeter falls.
   _____ if it snows more than a centimeter.

5. I never watch horror movies before bed. I just can't get to sleep!
   _____, I can't get to sleep.

B Rewrite the factual conditional sentences in Exercise A, reversing the clauses and using commas where necessary.

1. _I go jogging if it doesn't rain._
2. _____
3. _____
4. _____
5. _____

C Choose the correct form to complete each present or future factual conditional sentence.

1. If they (like / will like) the musical, they (see / will see) it again tomorrow.

2. Whenever Fernando (watched / watches) comedies, he (laughed / laughs).

3. If you (buy / will buy) some ice cream, I (help / will help) you eat it.

4. When I (won't / don't) fall asleep, I usually (get / got) a lot of work done in the evening.

5. (Will you / Do you) travel to England if your boss (needs / will need) you there next month?

6. Always (wear / wore) your seat belt if you (want / will want) to be safe.

7. I (didn't get / won't get) a tattoo if my parents (tell / told) me not to.

8. If I (ask / will ask) my brother for help, he (say / will say) no.

9. Whenever I (travel / will travel) far, I always (fly / flew) first class.

D Complete the sentences, using the appropriate possessive nouns.

1. The _____ tip is still on the table.
   waiter

2. _____ wallet was stolen when he was on vacation.
   Lucas

3. The _____ new computer cost them an arm and a leg.
   Browns

4. If the _____ team wins tonight, they'll be in the championships.
   women

5. They undercharged me for _____ present.
   Tom and Audrey

6. Whose money is this? Is it _____ ?
   Lucy

7. Whenever I travel, I borrow my _____ suitcase.
   parents

8. My aunt and uncle don't care for my _____ tattoo.
   cousin

E Answer the questions, using pronouns in place of the underlined nouns and noun phrases. The answers to the questions are in Unit 10. Check the Student's Book page in parentheses.

1. Did <u>Matt</u> break <u>the plate</u>? (page 111)

   Yes, he broke it.

2. Is <u>Matt</u> going to tell <u>the owner</u>? (page 111)

   _____

3. Did <u>the waiter</u> charge <u>the husband and wife</u> for <u>their desserts</u>? (page 113)

   _____

4. Did <u>a customer</u> return <u>the jacket</u> to <u>the child and her father</u>? (page 114)

   _____

5. Did <u>the homeless man</u> keep <u>the wallet he found</u>? (page 118)

   _____

6. Did <u>the "subway hero"</u> know <u>the passenger he saved</u>? (page 118)

   _____

7. Did <u>the airport screener</u> give <u>the bag of money</u> back to <u>its owner</u>? (page 118)

   _____

WRITING BOOSTER

A Choose a situation from page 119 of the Student's Book. Write the situation on the line.

_____

B On a separate sheet of paper, write a paragraph about what you could do in that situation, if you didn't act with kindness or honesty. For example, discuss the advantages of keeping money you found or not paying for something.

C Now write a second paragraph about what you should do in that situation. Begin your paragraph with <u>On the other hand</u>.

D Read your paragraphs. Circle the paragraph that describes what you think most people would do. Put a star next to the paragraph that describes what you would do.